Journeys Through Life Book 3

A True Story

Deep
Inside

Forgiving the Unforgivable.

Loving the Unlovable.

Tammy Horvath

TYH Publications

ISBN: 978-1-7368861-8-2 (Paperback on Amazon)

ISBN: 978-1-7368861-9-9 (Paperback on Publish Drive)

ISBN: 979-8-9895279-0-8 (eBook)

This book is a memoir. Dialogue has been recreated from memory, and people may remember it quite differently. Some names, places, and dates have been altered to protect the privacy of individuals and make the story more enjoyable; however, the details and creative dialogue are consistent with my memories. The author and publisher don't guarantee the accuracy of information in the book.

First edition published 2024.

Printed in the United States of America

TYH Publications

117 Forest Street, Sidman, PA 15955

CONTENTS

1. A Mother's Life Forever Changed

The day my son died, my life changed forever. Life, or possibly the devil, looked me in the face and said, "I dare you to get out of bed and face the day! You aren't strong enough. Your pain will be the death of you. You aren't capable of being loved or giving love." But like the Acacia tree in the Serengeti in Africa, I had deep roots in my faith. The tree can survive droughts because it has long roots deep in the ground where there is water. Even fire doesn't destroy the tree. It will grow again because of its strong roots. If I stayed rooted in Jesus, I knew he would give me strength to persevere. And then I'd resprout too, like the tree.

·♥·♥·♥·♥·♥·

When the doorbell rang shortly after midnight on August 3, 2017, I rushed to answer it, hoping the sound wouldn't wake my husband who was sleeping beside me. Three uniformed men stood on our porch. Entering our kitchen, they told me to sit down as my husband, Mike, came into the room. What happened next is something no mother should ever have to endure.

The officer looked at his notes. "According to Luke's friends, Tyrone and Luke were exchanging marijuana products, and Tyrone pulled a gun. He fatally shot your son point-blank."

Shortly after, based on testimonies provided by witnesses, officers arrested Tyrone.

I had been traumatized when Tony, Luke's dad and my first husband, died in a car accident when my son was one year old. Tony had ignored my preaching about not driving drunk, and he'd wrecked many cars before the accident that killed him. I found motherhood challenging, and when I met Mike, I was filled with joy. He became my rock and tried hard to be a great stepdad to Luke.

Had Mike not been there, I wouldn't have been strong enough to tell my parents their grandson was no longer with us. Mike helped with all those details and cared for me since I was so grief-stricken. But I saw his tears when he thought I wasn't looking.

I crumbled. Robotlike, I survived each day and made funeral arrangements. I had to call and tell family members what had happened, shocking them with the details the officers shared with me. By the time I ended each call, my shirt was soaked with tears.

I had to face giving my son's eulogy. Everyone told me I couldn't do it—that I wasn't strong enough. But I found strength in the challenge to prove them wrong. It would be my last gift to Luke. The childhood stories I shared about my little boy almost broke me. I cried and laughed while wishing I could travel back in time; I knew I'd remember that speech for the rest of my life. Everyone told me what a great job I did, but I had no choice. Someone had to do it. No one else wanted to.

·♥·♥·♥·♥·♥·

The judge banged her gavel. "Get him out of here! Now!" We had just finished the sentencing for Tyrone McDuffie, the young man who had murdered my only child, Luke Yuzwa. I had thought the sentencing would relieve some of my pain, but the courtroom ordeal only caused more stress. A row of seats was all that separated us.

"Get in touch with Nick and Andrew and make them tell you what happened!" Even though there was chaos everywhere, I could hear Tyrone's words clearly.

Nick and Andrew were with Luke when Tyrone robbed him and shot him over a drug deal gone wrong.

I thought I had all the answers for why my son was in Old Conemaugh Borough that August night. But apparently there was more to the story, and Luke's friends had the answers—so why hadn't they told me or the Assistant District Attorney?

·♥·♥·♥·♥·♥·

In the meantime, I needed to find a way to face my pain. God wanted me to feel his comfort, but that would only happen if I let him help me. Keeping busy, exercising, traveling, and enjoying God's beautiful creation were a few ways I learned to cope with the loss of my only child and come out stronger for it.

·♥·♥·♥·♥·♥·

My Transformational Journey

Just because Mike wasn't my son's biological dad didn't mean he didn't love Luke as much as I did. My heart wasn't the only one broken over Luke's death. I needed to pay attention to those around me and offer comfort when I felt up to it. Not everyone was as strong as me. God gave me strength for a reason, and he wanted me to help others process their grief.

I would also need to use this strength to find out the truth from Luke's friends. It would be challenging, but I'd do my best to make it happen. They were hiding something. I wanted to know what and why.

2. TRYING SOMETHING NEW CAN WORK WONDERS

Mike had been cycling for over a year, and I envied his muscular legs. We had a gym in our basement, and I worked out every morning. But I complained about the boredom of looking at the same four walls, so Mike had been bugging me to ride with him where nature's beauty awaited. Whoever said you never forget how to ride a bike was out of their mind. But I agreed to take his bike for a ride. The two curves in my spine that I had been born with were my biggest worry, so I hoped they wouldn't hurt while cycling. Every time I used my upper body for exercising, I'd cry from pain for at least two days. But I love my husband and like to do things with him, and what doesn't kill me only makes me stronger. And if it hurt too much, I could always quit.

Mike walked the bike to the side street near our house and held it for me to get on.

"Mike, I need to ride in the grass."

"You can't. It'll be too hard to pedal."

"Well, when I fall on the blacktop, that'll hurt too much, so grass it is." I pulled the bike out of his hands and walked into our yard.

Little did I know, Mike had his phone and was recording me. It took all my might to push the pedals after I climbed on and wobbled left and right, trying to control the bike in the rough terrain until I fell over.

"I told you I couldn't do it." Upset at my failure, I began to cry.

"You're going to love the video I made." I realized that our neighbors who rented the apartments we had in our backyard were watching. That made me feel even more embarrassed.

Mike didn't say anything else as we ate dinner. But I promised myself I'd figure out how to ride again.

·♥·♥·♥·♥·♥·

The last time I rode was in the third grade. Mike's niece, Amy, and I rode on that same road. We were chased by some boys, causing me to fall. Mike's brother John had to carry me to my gram, who lived next door to Mike. Gram called my mom, and we rushed to the hospital.

The doctor stared at the X-rays. I'd broken my arm and needed a sling.

After having the cast put on, I ran into my gram's arms and cried. I loved Gram dearly, and even at that age, I knew my accident had scared her.

"She must be careful and not use her arm for six to eight weeks. Possibly longer. Be sure she wears the sling to school, although she can take it off to sleep."

"OK. Thank you."

We left the hospital, and in the car, I saw my face in the rearview mirror. It was covered in bloody scratches, and my nose hurt. Mom raced home, worried about what my dad would say. My baby sister Jamie sat next to me. Music played from the radio as Mom flew around the turns, trying to cut off time from the twenty-five-minute trip.

Sirens blared, but Mom didn't slow the car. Finally, Gram said, "Mary Alice, I think he wants you to pull over."

"What? No. He can't be after me."

Tapping the brakes, Mom slowed the car and parked on the side of the road. Jamie gave a loud, piercing scream.

A uniformed police officer tapped on the driver's side window as Mom leaned over the back seat, trying to comfort my sister.

After Jamie stopped crying, Mom rolled down the window.

"Ma'am, do you know how fast you were going?"

"No. I don't. I'm sorry, was I speeding?"

"The speed limit is thirty. I clocked you doing fifty-five. That's almost double the limit."

"Oh my. I didn't mean to. My daughter just broke her arm. I'm trying to get her home to her dad."

Jamie chose this time to scream again. Being only three, who could blame her? She'd never had this much excitement in her life.

The man peered into the backseat, where he saw my arm in a cast and my bloody face probably turning black and blue. He must have had compassion for that young mother. "You can go. Take your kids home to their father. Just slow it down."

Mom took it slow the rest of the way home. It shocked Dad to hear I'd wrecked my bike. I was worried they wouldn't let me return to Gram's, afraid I might get into more trouble with my friend.

At school, a few friends carried my books, and I struggled to write even though I was right-handed and my left arm was broken. It was hard doing everything with one hand. But my classmates thought it was cool and signed my cast. I was popular. Yes! My cast remained on longer than expected because I kept falling on it. Like my sister, I was accident-prone.

Ten weeks later, my body froze when the doctor approached me with a circular saw. What did the doctor intend to do with the same kind of saw my dad used to cut large pieces of wood? "What's that for, Mom?" I pushed my head into her side, trying to make my body disappear.

The doctor looked at my face; it was full of fear. "Tammy, I know what I'm doing. I've done this many times, and I promise I won't hurt you."

No way! Surely he was joking. *Goodbye, world. This is it. I'm going to die.*

Tears rolled down my face as the nurse held my arm on the table—I tried to pull it away when I heard the loud saw roar to life. My body shook. Again, I used all my strength, but my arm wouldn't budge. My eyes pleaded with Mom to make the noise stop. Mom ran her hand through my hair, trying to comfort me. It didn't work. Mom held my gaze, and I knew she was trying to take the fear away. So I looked into her eyes, trying to find that comfort. But it didn't stop me from screaming when the blade made contact with my cast. But there was no pain; the cast was soon off, and Mom wiped my tears away.

·♥·♥·♥·♥·♥·

That was why I insisted on riding in the grass—I was terrified I'd break another bone. The next day, while Mike worked, I snuck the bike out of the garage, hiding from the security cameras. I planned to surprise him. So I practiced again on the grass. My legs hurt. It was so hard to pedal. I fell once but climbed back on, thinking the bumps in the yard had caused me to fall. *Dare I go out on the road?*

Gathering my courage, I cruised onto the road. There weren't any cars around. It was a rough, half-gravel, half-blacktop road that formed a circle in our small town. I rode to the ball field and back to the garage. It was only a few blocks away. Doing that daily while Mike was at work gave me confidence. And it also built up my leg muscles as I increased my repetitions every day.

One evening, several days later, after Mike returned from work and parked his truck in the garage, I yelled to him, "Mike, come outside. I've something to show you." After riding several hundred feet, I stopped in the driveway. Mike smiled, but he didn't seem surprised. "Aren't you excited?"

"Yes! I'm thrilled. But I knew you were practicing because I saw you on the Ring cameras." And I had tried so hard to avoid them. Oh well.

"Take me up to the windmills. I want to see this big hill you keep talking about."

"You won't be able to climb it yet. It's tough. I had to build my muscles for months before I could reach the top."

"I just want to see it. I don't want to climb it. At least not yet."

"It's not something you can just see. You have to climb it to see it. Let me get our water bottles, and I'll show you."

For the last year, Mike had been climbing the 847-foot hill on the gravel road, riding over six miles. Now it was my turn to show him what I was made of. Little did I know how hard it would be.

"The hill's so steep. I'm terrified to walk it, let alone ride it." My only option was to push my bike when I got to the steepest part. After cresting the worst part, I rode to the first gate. Ducking under the gate that kept cars out, we ignored the no trespassing signs as we rode further until my legs screamed in pain.

"I can't go any further, Mike. You can finish, but I'm going home to take ibuprofen."

Mike took me on several rides over the next month to build my muscles. We started using an app called Strava to track our activities. By the end of the month, I could climb to the top of the windmills, but I still walked my bike over the two very steep sections. Riding those would come in time.

·♥·♥·♥·♥·♥·

My Transformational Journey

Mike pushed me to be the best I could be. He wanted someone to cycle with, and I loved him, so I wanted to please him. Never one to enjoy nature, it shocked me to learn how relaxing it was riding on the trails in the middle of the trees. The fresh air usually relieved headaches, and I loved looking at flowers, animals, and waterfalls. I'd never known the views I missed by exercising in my gym while watching TV.

3. A Near-Death Experience

After not being around family for the holidays for well over a year because of what the CDC now called the horrible ongoing COVID-19 disease, Mom finally talked Mike and me into going for Thanksgiving. My sister and her family decided not to come, but I didn't know why. The food was delicious, but what I enjoyed most was seeing my aging parents. Because of their declining health issues, I needed to treasure moments and make memories while we could. Life is short.

After lunch, I helped clean up and loaded the dishwasher. Dad had retired to the garage to drink a Rolling Rock, his favorite beer, and Mom pulled Mike and me into a tight embrace before we walked out the door.

Mike was in the grass two steps in front of me, walking to our house next door. "Tammy, I wish your mom hadn't hugged us. I'm nervous enough around people since COVID is still rampant."

"I wasn't exactly happy about it either, but she hasn't seen us in a year and a half. What was I supposed to do?"

Mike opened the door to our house, and I put the leftovers into the fridge. That evening, we watched TV before heading to bed. Mike awoke at 4 a.m. and left for work, but I was a full-time writer and worked from home. Mom called around ten. "I'm not feeling well and don't want to make anyone sick at church in two days. I think I better get a COVID test."

"OK. Let me know the results." I called my sister. "Mom's going to get a COVID test since she doesn't feel well."

"I know. That's why we didn't come yesterday."

"What? You knew she was sick?"

"Yes."

My sister was a CAT scan technician at the hospital and couldn't afford to get sick because that would leave her coworkers short-staffed. And because of that never-ending pandemic, they were already working overtime to keep up with the influx of patients. *Why hadn't Mom told me she was sick?*

Mom's test was positive, and within a few days, she and my dad could barely take care of themselves. Since she had already exposed me to the deadly virus and I felt well, I shopped and bought them medicine and food, all while staying six feet away from everyone and wearing my mask. But on the fourth day, I woke up sick. Continuing to care for my parents had been at a price. By day five, I couldn't even get out of bed.

Mike popped his head into the bedroom. "How are you?"

"I'm sick. Every bone in my body hurts. My head feels like it's going to explode, and my stomach is upset. The bed is soaked, so I must have a fever. Can you bring me water and ibuprofen?"

Mike handed me two pills and a glass of water. He looked distraught. "I'm going to i-Care for a COVID test."

"Are you sick too?"

"I think so. I don't want to go to work and expose anyone."

I decided to go with him and also get tested. Mike struggled to drive the car to the clinic, and I couldn't drive because I couldn't sit upright. Lying on the bed while waiting for the nurse to take my test, I stared at Mike, pale and slumped in a chair. Exhausted, my eyes wouldn't stay open.

The door slamming startled me awake. Someone in a hazmat suit stood between Mike and me. "Who's first?"

Mike volunteered, and I watched as a long, tapered swab disappeared into his nose. His eyes watered. The nurse twisted the swab, and Mike's face spoke volumes. I'd heard how unpleasant those tests were, and I wasn't looking forward to my turn. Mike sneezed into his mask many times as I suffered the same invasion in my nose. We both fell asleep waiting for the results.

We left with our positive tests. Mike had been taking care of my parents' coal furnace, but after two more days, he called my dad and left a message that he could no longer do it. After several more days, we were both so weak that walking twenty feet to the bathroom was a struggle. We slept twenty hours each day, and I stopped eating. Mike continued eating Jello and drank lots of water, but I gagged every time I took a sip of the water. One of my son's friends dropped off Gatorade, and Mike's sister, Lyssa, brought us milkshakes from Sheetz. We tried to eat, but we just didn't have the strength.

Using the oxygen monitor his sister had dropped off, Mike said his levels were low, severely low—the machine read sixty-five. "I can't breathe. I need to go to the hospital."

"It won't do any good. Mom and Dad went yesterday, and after a twenty-hour wait, the doctor sent them home."

"I have to go. I can't breathe," Mike repeated. We didn't want to expose anyone to the virus, but we were too weak to drive. Mike called his sister Joan, a CAT scan tech who worked with my sister. She hung shower curtains in her SUV and picked us up at the house to take us to the hospital. We slouched in the back seat, staring at the stars. *Is this the end?*

The hospital only allowed the sick person to enter. No visitors were allowed. But since Mike and I were both sick, we went in together. Everything spun around me as I staggered through the door. A receptionist behind a glass wall checked us in, and a nurse took our blood pressure, temperature, and oxygen levels. She then escorted us into a room with a huge sign on the door that said "COVID patients only." We found two seats together, and the two-day wait began. At least, that's what we'd been told. People coughed and moaned. It sounded like we'd entered hell—that's how I pictured hell. A man constantly shouted, "Will someone help me? Please! I need a bed and a drink. Nurse!" Others snored as Mike and I tried to drown out the noise. A middle-aged woman came in and started watching loud videos on her phone. *How rude.* It was 2 a.m.

Finally, we fell asleep. A nurse woke Mike eight hours later. "The doctor said to put you on oxygen, since your levels are too low. We'll admit you soon and move you to a room once we have a bed. Your wife can't go with you."

Next, he checked me. After a thorough checkup, he asked about my symptoms.

"I haven't eaten or drunk in days, and I'm not leaving here without an IV." He agreed it would be beneficial and hooked me up with an IV as soon as he got Mike situated with this oxygen tank. The kind nurse brought me a blanket and pillow and gave me a pill for my nausea. Hours passed, and the nurse finally admitted Mike after a twenty-seven-hour wait. He hugged me goodbye, and I cried, not knowing if that would be the last time I'd see him. If the oxygen didn't work, the next step would be to put Mike on a ventilator. I'd heard horror stories that most intubated people died. Having already lost my first husband and my son, I was terrified that I was about to lose another loved one. Shivering, I pushed the thought to the back of my mind.

After I finished two IV drips, the doctor released me, and Joan took me home. All the way home I cried, devastated at being separated from Mike. I prayed Joan wouldn't get sick. But she knew what she was doing since she worked around COVID patients all day.

Tears soaked my pillow as I cried myself to sleep, worried I'd never see Mike again. My senses of taste and smell had left while I was in the hospital, but I forced myself to eat canned soup before eventually getting enough energy to make an enormous pot of chicken noodle soup from scratch. One day turned into two without Mike. Then three. Four. Five. Would I ever see him again? Finally, after one week in the hospital, the doctor sent Mike home, but he had to continue using oxygen for the next month. *Would we ever heal? Would life ever return to normal?*

My parents were doing well, except for the fact that some of my mom's hair had fallen out. She had terrible bald spots. When mine started falling out, I cut it all off, as Mom eventually did. She was blessed that her insurance provided her with a beautiful blond wig. It took one more month before life returned to normal.

·♥·♥·♥·♥·♥·

My Transformational Journey

COVID had changed me. Death had taken so much from me; I didn't want to lose anyone. I wanted to love and be loved again. When that terrible pandemic attacked Mike and me again in 2023, I learned from my previous mistakes. For the first twenty-four hours, I slept. Not eating or drinking made me weak, and when I lost my sense of taste and smell on the third day, I wanted to eat even less. But I forced myself to eat, take my vitamins, and drink plenty of fluids—especially Gatorade. Those actions made all the difference, and even though my hair again started falling out, I felt significantly better in three days. Learning from past mistakes is essential, and I'm glad I did. I pray this terrible virus goes away forever.

4. A Girls' Trip Gone Wrong

People always asked me if it was hard for me to see parents with their children. Knowing I shouldn't feel that way made me upset with myself for overreacting to a normal, everyday occurrence. A childhood friend and her sister accompanied me to my time-share at Massanutten in Virginia. It was a girls' trip. Booking two units, I thought they'd enjoy privacy. Near the end of the week, while playing games in their condo, they talked on Facetime with their children. There was lots of laughter and jokes, and I'd already drunk almost a bottle of wine. We had to check out in the morning, so I'd already loaded my car and had said I'd leave before they awoke. Excusing myself after the calls with their youngsters, I went to my room. Luke would never be with me again, and I longed to laugh with him as they did with their kids. The "I love you" at the end of the calls did me in. In my mind, I heard my son say, "I love you to the moon," just like he did at the end of all our calls. It was as if he was in the room with me, and I longed to hold him—but I couldn't. Sorrow consumed me.

Packing the rest of my things, I quickly left the condo, not bothering to tell anyone since I had no intention of making it home. I won't go so far as to say I was suicidal, but it would have been OK with me if I'd had an accident and didn't live through it.

My phone rang when my friends realized I'd left. When I didn't answer, my car played my friend's text message that followed the call. "Tammy, get your butt back here. Now!"

"I don't want to talk to anyone. Please leave me alone. I need space," was my reply. My pain was unbearable.

Her messages continued, and then her sister started texting too. They both loved me. That I knew, but I didn't care. My phone rang. It was my husband. Frustrated, I answered the sixth call.

"Tammy, what's going on? Why'd you leave without telling anyone? Are you on your way home?"

"Mike, life's too much. I can't take it. Everyone has their kids, and I don't. But your children are alive, so you don't know what losing a child is like."

"Tammy, please tell me where you are."

"No. I'm not coming home, and I'm turning off my phone, so quit bothering me. I'm sorry, but life is too much."

Pulling off the road, I searched the internet to turn off tracking on my phone. Then, I drove toward home a different way. Music blasted, sad music like "Dust in the Wind" by Kansas, "Anthem of the Angels" by Breaking Benjamin, and "If Today Was Your Last Day" by Nickelback. The bass vibrated the car, and I continued singing as loudly as possible. Wind from the open moonroof blew through my hair as I thought about reuniting with Luke. My baby blue Chrysler cruised on the highway doing 85 mph on route 81N. *Who cares if I get pulled over?*

Numerous calls and text messages blew up my phone since I didn't turn it off as I'd threatened. They cared about me. Scared, they didn't know what else to do. But I couldn't take it. Life was unbearable without Luke.

A car's high beams in my rearview mirror blinded me as it quickly approached, swerving in and out of the lane. My shaking hands gripped the steering wheel tighter. When the dark car was beside me, it nearly sideswiped me and then disappeared in a few minutes. Tears soaked my cheeks and neck because I thought that was it. But God had other plans.

A red-lighted cross glowing in the dark stood on the opposite side of the highway. I couldn't take my eyes off it. A few miles up the road, when I wiped tears from my eyes, I noticed several cars were stopped. My Chrysler activated the Forward Collision Warning System, and I held my breath as I quickly approached the rear end of a tractor-trailer. It was then that I realized I didn't want to die. Joyous tears poured as I remembered the cross—God's sign that he was still with me and would get me through the hard days ahead of living without my son.

When I walked into the kitchen at home, my husband embraced me. It was two a.m. He hugged me tighter and refused to let go. "I'm so glad you're OK. Don't ever scare me like that again, because I don't want to lose you." Snuggled tight in his arms, I slept soundly until the sun arose, giving me peace. The previous night, Mike had texted my friend to let her know I was OK when he'd seen my car pull into the garage. *How did I deserve this wonderful man?*

·❤·❤·❤·❤·❤·

Now I was ready to talk. My friend didn't answer the phone when I tried to call her. Instead, she replied to my messages that she was busy and didn't have time to stop and see me as I'd asked. It wouldn't go over well on the phone if I tried to explain what happened when I had left the time-share without telling her. Just as well, it needed to be done in person.

Mike and I were invited to a picnic, and I knew she'd be there. Sitting next to her at the picnic table with many people wasn't my first choice of a perfect location. But I was upset with myself for what had happened, so I did my best to explain how my feelings of missing Luke had caused me to react in an unhealthy way.

But with everyone listening, I only said, "I'm sorry I upset you and didn't talk to you about my feelings. I understand if you don't want to be friends anymore."

"Tammy, we'll always be friends. Everyone has problems. Friends love each other despite their problems."

"OK. Thanks for forgiving me."

"Sure. No problem." She hugged me tightly.

But I had a feeling she didn't truly understand. We haven't hung out since, and months later, she posted something on Facebook about missing her mom since she had recently passed and was now in heaven. For everyone to see, I responded to that post and explained everything I was going through on the night I wanted to end my life.

She replied to my comment. "I didn't know you were going through all that." When I explained it at the picnic, I knew she didn't understand the depth of my grief, but it was too hard to talk with so many people around. I'll do better in the future to make sure I keep the few genuine friends that I have. It's been one and a half years, and we still haven't hung out. Maybe I blew it for good.

·♥·♥·♥·♥·♥·

My Transformational Journey
When I'm sad or suicidal, I must remember to listen to uplifting music. Listening to songs about someone dying or life being meaningless will only make things worse. Instead, I could have listed everything I was thankful for, like Mike and my family and friends who love me. My friends were there for me, but I pushed them away instead of asking for help. And God was waiting for me to turn to him too. Even though I felt unlovable, Jesus loved me. And still does.

5. Why Did I Shoot the Mattress?

When I got home from Virginia, I set our home alarm, but it kept turning off. Something was wrong. Poor Mike. My husband had installed the system when we got married because I was terrified someone was trying to hurt me. It all started after my first husband had died, and I feared being alone in the house with Luke—that's when I got my first alarm.

I'd inherited my late husband's fieldstone business at the time of his passing. Since Tony was the one who ran the company, I had no choice but to step up to the challenge. But most of the work was completed in the woods using a front-end loader, which was dangerous in itself and also dangerous because there were snakes. So I couldn't be there constantly with my one-year-old son, and my income wasn't enough to pay for childcare. The business was quite new, and after paying the bills, there wasn't any profit left. In stepped Mr. Newhire, my husband's mechanic. I had met him when he had stopped at our home frequently to drop off repair bills for my husband and had thought him to be obnoxious. He could have woken the dead with his loud voice that made me cringe—like fingernails on a chalkboard.

Everything happened quickly, and this man stepped into our lives for good when my loader had a flat tire. He met me at the job site and, besides fixing the tire for free, offered to help Luke and me with anything we needed. I was alone. Scared. A single mother. But the man rubbed me the wrong way. Even so, I panicked and called him when my 1995 Mazda 626 wouldn't start. After fixing a loose wire, he dropped a tool on his hand. "Crap," he yelled, but in a much more colorful way. I especially hated it when he swore in front of Luke. But that didn't stop me from asking him to become my foreman—I had no choice. I needed someone qualified to supervise the employees, and I also needed a mechanic.

The man knew the way to my heart. It started when he took Luke and me out for dinner almost every night after work. Then he started paying for a babysitter, so he had time alone with me. His voice was so loud that it embarrassed me when he complimented me publicly. He didn't know how to whisper, even after I begged him.

Luke squealed when Mr. Newhire's truck pulled into the driveway, knowing he would play with him, usually by wrestling with him and throwing him on the couch repeatedly. My son screamed with delight. Luke loved him so much that he cried every time he left. The three of us took long lunches while the employees worked. My mechanic brought flowers for me and toys for Luke, along with many other gifts. He even fixed my dad's truck when it needed brakes.

"How can you stand being around that man?" Dad was putting his tools away after Mr. Newhire had left. "He's so loud."

"I know. But he helps with anything I need done." Dad didn't know the half of it.

My foreman bought groceries, paid for gas, and gave me cash when needed. He even hired someone to cut my grass every week. Lonely and wanting a father figure for my son, the walls I'd built around my heart after losing Tony started to crumble. When I was in the room with Mr. Newhire, I had his undivided attention. He made me feel the same way Tony had when I first met him. After hitting on me for several months, he kissed me. And I let him. Tears poured from my eyes; I was worried I was cheating on Tony. But he was gone. I had to move on with life. I finally gave in and started dating this man who had slowly wormed his way into our lives. Mr. Newhire was kind and devoted to Luke and me. Soon, I fell in love with him, and he said he loved me too. I was the happiest I'd been since Tony's death. Life was perfect.

Several months later, I discovered he had another family—a woman and their kids. He said he wasn't married to the woman and was leaving her, but he still lived with her.

However, when I eventually met her, she was very nice. I liked her. We got to talking, and she said they were married. Why had the man I loved deceived me? I needed to break things off. And quickly. Not wanting to wreck their home, I tried to spend less time with him. But since he ran the business, it became problematic when he created reasons we needed to be together. He made me go with him on several trips to sell fieldstone in the states surrounding Pennsylvania. Very much in love, it broke my heart that I couldn't be with him. He was the first man I had gotten serious with since my husband died. And he had manipulated me into thinking I needed him.

When I started dating another man, hoping the mechanic would get the message, Mr. Newhire showed up at my house and started a fight. I had to call the cops to break it up. The situation was getting violent, and I feared for our safety. Then, someone started making noise on my three-sided wrap-around deck in the middle of the night. The nightly footsteps went on for months. When I told Mr. Newhire about it, he told me to page him when it happened. Instead of entering my phone number, he said to enter 911, and he'd come immediately. I still loved the man and didn't know where to turn when I was scared, so I paged him. Many times, he showed up in five minutes. That was odd because he lived thirty minutes away.

One stormy night, I heard the noise and was terrified. But instead of paging my knight in shining armor, I called the cops. An officer arrived at my house but didn't find anyone lurking, so he left. After that, the officer started doing routine drive-bys to check on me.

When I told Mr. Newhire I'd called the cops, his expression spoke volumes. "I told you to page me. So why did you call the cops?"

"I can't keep bothering you. You have your own family, and you shouldn't have to worry about Luke and me."

He stomped off, going back to work. His reaction was a little strange. My phone call to 911 had upset him way too much, and I became frightened of him.

The deck activity increased. Terrified, I didn't know what to do. Sometimes I called my neighbor when I saw their lights were still on and asked if they could see anyone outside my house. When that didn't work, I called my brother-in-law, who came over. No one could find the culprit. Even one of my first husband's friends who lived nearby rushed over. It was all useless. Whoever it was avoided detection.

Losing sleep, I had to find another solution. Finally, one night, I decided enough was enough. *When it happens again, I will stop this once and for all.* Tony had owned a .38 Special that I'd inherited when he died. But I wasn't sure I would use the gun even if I felt threatened.

·♥·♥·♥·♥·♥·

My Transformational Journey

I knew I needed to be brave to protect my son. But the only time I had ever handled a gun was when Dad took me to shoot a rifle when I was a teenager. That was fun. But Dad had loaded the cartridges, so I was clueless about how to operate it. Even though Tony's handgun was smaller, it terrified me. One year after Tony and I had married, he'd stayed out all night, and I heard a noise in the house. After removing the revolver from its holster on the nightstand next to my bed, I pulled the hammer back, ready to shoot. After I was sure no one was in the house, I tried to decock the loaded revolver but ended up shooting into the mattress. I never told anyone about it.

6. A Security System Controlled by a Stalker

When I next heard the footsteps outside, I was ready. Grabbing the gun and my keys, I slipped on my shoes in the dark and quietly shut and locked the door behind me. The sensor light on my garage shone brightly, meaning someone had been there in the last five minutes. Luke was sleeping in his crib, and I needed to protect him. The keys wouldn't be safe on my body because if the person attacked me, I didn't want them to have access to the house, so I threw them in the grass. Then, creeping quietly through my grapevine arch, I slid my back along the house wall, climbing one step at a time. I was almost at the first corner of the wooden deck.

The nearby streetlight illuminated the deck around the turn, but that didn't calm my shaking body. Raising the gun, I pointed it upward as both my hands grasped it, as I had seen Farrah Fawcett do many times on the TV show *Charlie's Angels*. Sweat poured even though the temperature was only in the forties. I quickly peeked around the corner. My heart beat like a jackhammer as I pulled back and rested my head on the house siding.

Am I crazy? I shouldn't be doing this.

Since I hadn't seen anyone, I took a few deep breaths and turned the corner, racing across the deck to the next corner. A car's headlights shone as it passed my front deck. *Had someone been there, wouldn't they have run when the vehicle appeared?* I turned the next corner in a crouching position and was on my front deck. The railing hid my view from the road. No one was there.

After crossing the deck, I descended the steps and walked up the sidewalk to the back door. Next to my concrete slab patio, I moved my hands across the cold grass in search of my keys. Checking the back of the house one last time to make sure it was clear, I unlocked the door and entered the kitchen. After securing the deadbolt, I fell to the floor. Tears flowed for the next half hour.

The next morning, I greeted my employees before they started their day. Mr. Newhire looked tired. "Did you have any problems last night?" he asked.

"No. Why? Did someone see something?"

"I haven't heard from you for a few nights and wondered if you want me to sleep over tonight?"

"Thanks. But a friend is staying with me tonight." Of course, lying wasn't the best option, but it was all that popped into my mind.

That night, Mr. Newhire showed up at 11:00 p.m. He was drunk.

If I let him in, it would be easy to fall back into old habits. "Go home to your family."

My heart still longed to be with him and to feel the love he had shown Luke and me for many months. But that couldn't happen. Why would someone want to have two families anyway? Tears fell as I listened to his truck pull out of my driveway. How I ever fell in love with him in the first place was beyond me. He was loud and obnoxious. Few people liked him—my dad especially. He had been slowly worming his way into my life from the moment I had hired him to run the business. Weak from my loss, I was emotionally unstable. Mr. Newhire had deceived me. He already had a family, and, based on what his wife insinuated, he had no intentions of leaving them. It broke my heart that Luke, too, had a bond with this terrible man.

The same thing happened for several more nights. My intruder stalked me on my deck, and I searched for him with my gun. There was no standoff. There was no peace.

Finally, while on a business trip with Mr. Newhire, I told him I was trying to catch my intruder with Tony's revolver. He appeared shocked but said nothing.

·♥·♥·♥·♥·♥·

My doorbell rang at lunchtime after I set a hot bowl of stew on the table for Luke. Mr. Newhire stepped into the kitchen. "You won't have any more trouble with the man on your deck."

"What? Why? Did you find him?"

"Yes. It was your neighbor, Thad."

"No! How do you know that?"

"I confronted him, and he admitted it. Please don't go anywhere near him. He's dangerous. I threatened him and told him to stay away from you. He won't bother you again."

Shocked. I didn't know what to say. "Do you need anything else? I need to feed Luke. He's hungry." Averting my eyes, I looked at the floor.

After he tried to sit at my kitchen table, I opened the door and motioned for him to leave. He said goodbye to Luke and walked out as my son screamed for him to come back.

He couldn't be right about Thad—my neighbor wouldn't do that. When my toilet was leaking, it was Thad who fixed it. When my lawnmower wouldn't start, it was Thad who saved the day. When I screamed because a snake slithered through the grass, who came running to help? Thad. Thad was my hero. Not my tormentor.

Maybe Thad drank occasionally, and I sometimes heard him fighting with his sweet wife. But deep in my heart, I knew Thad was not my stalker.

·♥·♥·♥·♥·♥·

Mr. Newhire and I were leaving on a day-long business trip. We were loading my SUV with sample rocks to show to potential buyers. Luke screamed for me to put him down as I tried to put him in his car seat. I had just set the house alarm and realized I had forgotten the diaper bag. The alarm's delay was still chiming. When I told my employee, he asked for the code and the key and went to retrieve the bag. Remember, I still loved this man, and at that moment, I didn't think about the stupidity of giving him the alarm code.

But then I thought a little more about it. This man had lied to me about having another family. So why should I trust him? That lie was a big deal. And the fact that he appeared upset when I called the cops about my intruder concerned me even more. Why would he be upset because I called the cops instead of paging him? It was the police's job to help people. When I realized my mistake, that I shouldn't have given him the code, I reminded myself to change it the following day.

We spent a long day making sales for the business, and then I picked up Luke from my mom's. At home, I set the alarm, and we went to bed. Exhausted, I slept soundly and woke up rested. When I went to turn off the alarm, it had already been disabled. The power hadn't gone out; even if it had, there was a battery backup. So someone had been in my house or was still there. I quickly searched, carrying my .38 Special like Farrah Fawcett, while Luke slept. No one was in the house. *What a relief!*

The only thing that was out of place was the carpet on the closet floor of my bathroom. Under that carpet was access to the basement. But the basement had no windows, and there was a padlock on the door. After checking that the padlock hadn't been tampered with, I put my fears aside and wondered if I might have forgotten to set the alarm. But I knew I set it because I was terrified of whoever was trying to hurt us. I was so scared that I even set the alarm when we were home during the day. Still, I questioned my sanity and let it go.

But my mind kept returning to what Mr. Newhire had said about confronting my neighbor. What seemed odd was how he told me not to go near Thad. Could my employee be my stalker? No! It couldn't be him. But I needed to know, and there was only one way to find the truth.

When I saw Thad in his front yard a few hours later, I walked over. "How are you, Thad? How's your family?"

"We're well. How are you and Luke? Is there something I can help with?"

"I have a strange question. Do you know the guy who always works on my car and helps me around the house?"

"Yes. He drives a white truck, right?"

"Yes. Well, you know how I told you someone keeps walking on my deck in the middle of the night trying to break in or scare me?"

"Yes. I remember you telling me about it. On the scanner the other night, I heard about your call to 911."

"Did my friend talk to you the other day?"

"No. Why would he? Is there something I can help him with? Are you OK?"

Now, if Thad was the one who was walking on my deck and my employee had talked to him and threatened him as he said he did, I don't think my neighbor would have been as calm as he was when I walked over. And I don't think he would have been concerned if I needed help or if Luke and I were OK. So when I told him what my employee said happened, I believed him when he said he would never do that and that he was with his wife then. "You can talk to her. She'll vouch for me."

My employee had lied to me. Not only had he made Luke and me fall deeply in love with him, but he had tried to scare me into letting him back into our lives. Scaring a single mother is such a nasty thing to do—a mother who is trying to protect her child from danger at all costs. There's no way that Mr. Newhire had ever really cared for me if he could do something like that. He only had one reason to lie to me—he was the culprit, my stalker. And then I remembered he had the key to the padlock in my basement so he could have gotten into the house, and I had forgotten to change the security code. *How stupid am I?* He'd been manipulating me for months, first to fall in love with him and give him the salary he requested from the business, and then to make me feel like Luke and I needed him in order to feel safe. *I'm so mad at myself for not seeing this sooner.*

♥ · ♥ · ♥ · ♥ · ♥

My Transformational Journey

There were many gangs in our area, but I had no reason to think Luke's murder had anything to do with a gang. Unfortunately, there have been many occasions where I let my emotions lead my thinking instead of looking at the facts presented to me. Or asking God to protect me. Still, Mike needed to fix our security system. Today. Otherwise, I would not sleep.

7. A Murderer Caught on Camera

"I'm so sorry."

"Who is this? And why are you saying you're sorry? I'm Luke Yuzwa's mom. This was the last number my son called me from right before he was murdered Wednesday evening."

Unfortunately, it took days to get through to whomever I spoke to. Apparently, the person knew who I was, but had yet to enlighten me about who he was and why he was sorry.

Through tears, he finally told me his name was Nick.

"I'm so sorry." He repeated those words at least five times through gasping breaths.

Four days previously, my son had called me to pick him up so he could come home, get a few things, and then return to Nick's house.

"Luke, I'm exhausted."

"It's all good. I'll figure it out. I love you to the moon."

"I love you too." After hanging up, I hit play on my paused TV recording.

After Luke's murder, and just an hour after I'd spoken to Nick, Luke's long-time friend Jayme sat with me on my front porch and told me what happened next. Luke had called him just after I spoke to him. "Can you give me a ride home from my homies and then back?"

"Sure. Give me fifteen minutes, Luke."

"OK. I'll be standing by the grocery store on the corner of Railroad Street in Conemaugh."

One hour after I had talked to Luke, Jayme pulled into our driveway. Jayme later told me that Luke had said, "I need to grab $1,200 to buy a gun from a guy, and I need my phone charger because my phone just died again."

I had heard Luke run through the house, say hello to his cat, and leave quickly. He was gone so fast that I didn't see him.

Jayme continued. "On the way back to town, Luke dug in his backpack. I saw a huge machete, and Luke said he had it for protection. He also said he had homies in Conemaugh, but it wasn't enough. He needed a gun to feel safe."

Within four hours, at 9:30 p.m., Luke had been fatally shot at point-blank range with a semi-automatic weapon in an Old Conemaugh Borough, Pennsylvania street. His cause of death was a gunshot wound to the head. Nick and Andrew were with him when the robbery happened. The gunman ran off with Luke's backpack, and the police contacted me several hours later, saying they had the killer in custody. They charged twenty-two-year-old Tyrone McDuffie with criminal homicide, robbery, and possessing a stolen, unlicensed firearm.

Life stopped when I lost my only child, but the world kept turning for those around me. Birds chirped, and kids laughed outside, playing in the sun, but for me, my mind locked me in darkness. I went through the motions of living, eating minimally, occasionally showering, and answering all the many phone calls I received about the funeral arrangements. I'd shut down. Numb. I felt dead inside. Lost. Lonely. Broken.

My husband didn't know what to do for me. A single lonely tear no one saw remained, but I felt it lingering and knew they'd never end. Mike kissed my forehead and tucked my hair behind my ear. I pushed him away, worried I'd lose him too. I needed to be alone—I couldn't risk losing anyone again. With fear in my eyes, I looked at him as I put up walls to protect myself.

Later, Mike made soup and begged me to eat—he was my rock and the only reason I was still alive. There was no comfort as I sat for hours in bed, wishing I'd been there to jump in front of that single bullet to save my son—the love I could never replace. *Why couldn't it be me who died? Not him.* I cried out to God. *Why, God? Why him? Why not me?*

Every morning, I'd wake up and wait for Luke to come down the stairs. And every day when it didn't happen, I'd remember all the last moments. Our last dinner. Our last hug. And the last words he'd ever said to me when I'd told him I was too tired to give him a ride.

That conversation helped get me through those dark days. Knowing my son loved me and knowing I'd told him I loved him, too, helped me deal with my grief. Unfortunately, I knew little about the murder, and Nick was in no condition to help fill in the details I so desperately needed. The police had told me Andrew said the killer was trading marijuana for Luke's THC capsules and pot brownies. But I knew that wasn't true.

At least the murderer had been caught quickly and was held without bond behind bars at the Cambria County Prison. The gunman's criminal history included drug arrests and a guilty plea for a connection with a treatment facility riot that had injured employees, for which he'd served two years in state prison.

Over the next few years, I got to know Nick and visited him at his dad's house or gave him rides to work. He shared intimate details about the month leading up to the murder. "We spent hours working in the woods behind your house, clearing bushes and rock so we could make a lean-to out of sticks. We made a dam in the creek so we could swim. Luke was happy in the woods—he loved being at one with nature."

I'd known this about my son, but I cherished those words, knowing my son was happy. But my son was always careless with keys and money in his pockets, and one day, we'd spent two hours searching the woods trying to find the $100 he'd lost. My son was angry about the situation. He said, "Things always happen to me." Teaching him to be more responsible was impossible. I even bought wood so he could build a cabin in the trees. When he came out of the woods, his face could light up a room.

Nick lit a cigarette before continuing. "We both loved to play basketball. So after going to Sheetz and getting hamburgers and blue Slushies, Luke insisted on playing ball even though the sun was hot. We'd spend hours on the court. Luke was an excellent shot, and since he was tall and skinny, he was great at quick maneuvers."

I treasured my time with Nick and loved the many occasions when he unexpectedly brought up precious memories of Luke.

Nick tapped his cigarette over the ashtray on the table. "We played *Super Mario* on the Nintendo in your basement. We had a blast. Luke liked to play pool and dreamed of winning a trophy like his dad, so we practiced for hours, but he was so much better than me. Unfortunately, he beat me quickly, so it wasn't much of a challenge for him to improve his game. But when I had a problem, I knew Luke would listen without judging me. His ear was always there, and I knew it." Smoke rose from the cigarette in his hand.

"Nick, please tell me what happened when Luke was killed." Years had passed, and I still didn't know the whole truth.

"It's like I already told you."

"Which was?"

Nick looked deep in thought as he took a sip of water before continuing. "Luke went home to get his kief to trade for Xanax from Tyrone. We didn't want to do the deal in the house because the owner had cameras. So Tyrone said we could make the exchange behind his garage. We left. Luke and Tyrone were walking ahead of Andrew and me when Tyrone shot Luke in the head and ran off with his backpack."

After clearing my throat, I used my shaking hand to wipe a single tear that ran down my cheek.

"What's kief?" I'd never heard that word before.

"It's a sticky substance Luke kept in jars. He extracted it from pot."

That brought back memories of all the times I had scrubbed my dishes, trying to get the yellow gooey substance off them.

"I remember trying to scrub globs of sticky stuff from the carpet in his room. I never got it clean. We had to replace the carpet after he passed."

This story differed from the original one the police had told me Andrew had testified. *Will I ever get the answers? Will God ever show me the truth?*

"Can you tell me about Luke's emotional state the day he died?" My heart longed to know if he was happy. Or if he thought he was in danger.

"Luke was free stylin' and laughing. His favorite rapper was Tupac. But Luke said that rappers always sing about stuff they've never experienced, and he didn't want to be like that, so he rapped about what we did that day hanging out at my place. He was good at it."

"I wish I could've heard it." A tear slid down my face, thinking about the joy it would have given me.

Nick extinguished his cigarette in the ashtray. There were tears in his eyes.

"He also rapped about the used Audi you'd bought him."

"Oh, I loved that car. Too bad he only got to drive it for a week before the transmission went, and we got rid of it."

I opened my purse to look for a tissue.

"You sharing this with me means a lot, Nick."

"Luke was happy on his last day. He loved you. That I know." Nick pulled me into a tight embrace. "Goodbye. I'll see you soon."

It made me happy talking about Luke and spending time with his friends. Luke had been a great friend to everyone he'd met. He loved helping people, just like me, and he did that by being a good listener without casting judgment.

·♥·♥·♥·♥·♥·

My Transformational Journey

Talking about my son helped me to keep Luke alive in my heart. After losing a loved one, some people are the opposite. But since I knew it helped me heal, I needed to continue sharing stories with everyone who knew my son so that my heart would heal and hopefully find peace.

8. Lost Cycling in the Woods

Exercising kept my brain and body healthy, so my husband showed me his long cycling routine since I'd insisted that my muscles were strong enough to complete what he called The Loop. The first segment started with climbing to the windmills before riding down the steep hill of Dunlo Dip Road, which connected to a gated dirt road leading into the old Cooney Brothers strip mines. Riding through the strip cut was more straightforward than the workout I got climbing the 800 feet to the windmills. I took full advantage of the wind, which helped dry my sweat-soaked clothes. We rode miles into the middle of nowhere. Not another person around. Peaceful.

But that didn't last long as the sky grew dark, and we heard thunder in the distance. Mike rushed me along the route. After making three turns, it grew darker when I left the security of the wide dirt path, and we rode into the grass and dirt-covered hill leading into the woods. Wind blew the trees sideways, and leaves fell to the ground. My thin Cannondale Quick CX bike tires fought for control of my handlebar as I rode over several rocks. Unlike Mike, I didn't jump the front wheel over the small tree branch. Instead, I stopped abruptly, almost flipping into a somersault when I slammed on the brakes. Lifting my bike safely over the six-inch limb, I looked down the hill to see how much further I had to endure this challenging terrain. With no more downed trees in my path, I laughed as I zipped through a field, watching bees buzz in the flowers.

Tapping my brakes, I avoided a chipmunk running out of the tall bushes that brushed my legs. Mike stopped ahead, waiting for me.

"So, you had fun, did ya?"

"It was scary."

"I heard you laughing."

I brushed the dirt off my leg as I thought about how to answer him. "Yes. You're right. I'm proud of myself. How much further is it?"

"The next part is difficult because, along with rocks, you'll have to ride over more branches."

Did he think I was Superman? I didn't have near the upper body strength that he had.

"I didn't even ride over the last one. I stopped and lifted my bike."

"Just yank up hard on the handlebar and lean back so the front tire lifts slightly off the ground."

Rolling my eyes, I looked at the cloudy sky.

"Won't I tip backward off my bike?"

"No. You'll get the hang of it."

"OK." I didn't think I could do it, but I'd try.

Following him through the trees, the single-track dirt trail went up a steep hill, only to drop back down on the other side, reminding me of a roller coaster. When I saw the first tree branch before me, I did as Mike had instructed. But my tire didn't lift. My bike came to a sudden stop when the tire hit the limb.

"Whoa!" I fell sideways, and my foot twisted on a rock, but all was well. After getting my balance, I resumed my ride. *I'll try one more time over the next branch, and if it doesn't work, I'm done. Here goes.* With all my might, I pulled back. Hard. "I did it! Yay! Mike, I did it!"

Mike sat ahead on the trail and pointed his iPhone at me, recording my first ride through the woods. "I knew you could do it."

I didn't think he really thought that—he was just trying to encourage me.

While making a final dip into a turn, I almost wiped out as I came up the other side of the hill and went airborne. "Yippee!" Happy I hadn't wrecked, I smiled as my bike rolled into a field at the crest of the Lloydell Dam. The only trail left was one I'd ridden several times already, and it was a piece of cake. Then I'd need to conquer my fear and ride the two miles on the state road to our house as cars whipped by going 40 mph while my bike went at a slower pace of 22 mph. Glad I was wearing a helmet, I clung to the handlebar when a tractor-trailer whizzed by too close for comfort. According to Strava, riding the fourteen-mile loop had taken over two hours.

"Honey, I'm proud of you. Your time was phenomenal." Mike captured a selfie of us to remember that moment.

·♥·♥·♥·♥·♥·

One day, while Mike was at work, I rode The Loop. I planned to complete the reverse route since I didn't want to climb 800 feet to the windmills. Flying up the state road with my helmet securely fastened, I was happy my bike's red light blinked as cars passed me in the other lane. Exhilarated that I'd made great time getting to the Lloydell Dam, I knew Mike would be proud. While drinking from my water bottle, I looked for the trailhead to start my roller coaster adventure. I recalled that last time I almost wrecked when I came out of a dip and turned before entering the field I was now standing in—but that had happened so fast that I couldn't remember what the trail looked like.

Two single-track trails went to the right, and one two-lane went straight ahead. Riding to the right, I came to a standstill because a huge downed tree spread across the dirt path. Limbs and all. This didn't look right. So I turned around.

Choosing the two-lane path that looked like tire tracks, I pedaled extremely hard to make it through the overgrown grass and up the slight gradient. *You're fine, Tammy. At least you don't have to climb to the windmills. You got this.* Shortly after the top of the hill, I came to two enormous puddles. They spread across most of the tracks. Contemplating what to do, I listened to birds chirping in the trees as the wind blew my hair off my face, giving me a cooling break. This trail didn't look right. *I'll go a little further and turn back if it doesn't jog my memory.*

Testing the mud between the two puddles, I placed my sneaker on the edge. It sunk but soon stopped. Looking to the right of the trail, I saw a steep mountain; to the left, trees blocked any chance of getting through. So I had no choice but to walk through the wet mess. OK. My plan was to run as fast as I could in the mud while pushing my bike in the puddle to the left since it didn't look as deep. After taking a deep breath, I went for it. Three steps and my bike pulled me to a halt as it sunk deep into the black mud. A toad made the strangest noise as it moved across the rocks. My feet lowered in the dirty water to my shins as I tried to pull the bike out. Concerned about bugs and other things that may have been in the mud, I gave way to tears. It took all my strength to lift the bike. But I couldn't move. Now my feet were stuck.

Tossing the bike to the edge of the puddle ahead, I regretted my decision to exercise that day. Wiggling, twisting, and turning ensued for several minutes. One foot finally broke free from what felt like quicksand. Standing on one foot, I thought about my next move. Stretching to my max, I completed a 180-degree turn and placed the freed foot on a rock. Now to get the other one free. After much pulling with my hands on my knee, I was free. I jumped across the rest of the puddle to face my next problem. I knew I was headed the wrong way. But there was no way back. And I wasn't going back through that puddle.

Pulling my phone from my pocket, I knew I needed to tell Mike where I was. But there was no signal. The trail was a mess, and I had to push my bike. Only occasionally could I ride. I finally came to a field and was glad for the break. Scared. Alone. And lost. The sun wrapped me in a much-needed warm embrace. At the end of the field, the trail divided. The path I was supposed to take originally went to the right of this trail, so I went right. There was barely enough room for me and my bike as I pushed it up the steep, rocky terrain along the mountain's edge. The other trail appeared flat, but who knew where I'd end up? My back tire slid over the edge when I slipped. Landing on my butt, I pulled the bike partially onto my lap. *Tammy, pay more attention to your actions, or you'll break a bone. And no one knows where you are. And sure, Tammy, keep talking to yourself because it's really helping.*

At the top of the mountain, I had cell service, so I called Mike. But he didn't answer. I waited five minutes, and still no answer. My call went straight to voicemail. Mike's sons bike these trails, so I called Alan even though I knew he was at work.

"Alan. Listen to me in case I lose signal. I can't reach your dad; I'm biking and lost. The trail started above the Lloydell Dam, and I went straight instead of right. Do you understand me?" Afraid I'd lose signal, I wanted to spit that out in case I needed a search party to look for me later.

"Tammy, you need to turn around."

I looked behind me.

"No. I can't. You don't understand what I went through. I can't go back through the swamp, and I'm scared I'll fall if I try to go back down the mountain."

"I want you to turn around."

"No. It's too dangerous. Besides, I've been on this trail for over an hour. It has to lead somewhere. I've got to be close."

"OK."

"Just let your dad know where I am if you don't hear from me."

The call dropped as soon as I started walking. Something growling in the woods raised the hair on my arms. Standing still, I looked all around. *Are there bears here?* A branch cracked nearby—nothing but trees all around me. The sky was blue, and the white clouds looked so welcoming. *I wish I were on a plane to the beach. I'd give anything for that to be true.* The sound of birds chirping relaxed me, and I rubbed my shoulders and neck to get the kinks out.

The trail leveled off again, and I remounted my bike. Pedaling like a woman on a mission, I finally came to a clearing and saw a road ahead at the top of the next hill. My legs gave out and cramped halfway up the rocky path. Pushing my bike onto the dirt road, I collapsed at the edge. There were windmills in the distance to the right. The left went up a little hill, but I couldn't see over the top. Remembering that the original correct trail was to the right, I rode toward the windmills. Dust formed behind me as I forced my aching legs to resume the workout. *Never again. From now on, I won't ride any trails Mike hasn't ridden with me several times.*

My phone had service again, so I called Mike as I rode. He was terrified for me. "Mike, it's OK. The worst is over. At least I'm on the road again. I'll let you know as soon as I see a landmark."

When I finally figured out where I was, I sat on a rock behind the gate next to Dunlo Dip Road. Mike met me in his work truck. "Let me take you home."

"No. I need to finish this."

"At least let me drive you to the top of the hill."

Knowing I wouldn't make it up the hill since my legs were severely cramped, I agreed. No pedaling was needed to ride down the windmill's six-mile gravel trail to our house. I at least wanted credit on Strava for my terrible ordeal. I was born a fighter.

· ♥ · ♥ · ♥ · ♥ · ♥ ·

My Transformational Journey

It was stupid not to let anyone know where I was going. Strava has a free feature where you can ask the app to track you and send your signal to anyone. Now, anytime I cycle alone, I text my husband with the location beacon so he can follow me.

9. Waiting Six Years to Meet My Son's Killer

From the time Luke was murdered in August 2017, I'd contemplated meeting with his killer even though no one, including my family and friends, thought it was a good idea. While Tyrone was still in the local jail waiting for sentencing in 2020, I knew time was running out before he'd be moved further away. The caring prison captain sent messages between us, telling Tyrone I wanted to meet. When Tyrone agreed to see me, the captain said he would do everything possible to make it happen. But it was out of his control, so it was up to me to get the required permission from the Cambria County District Attorney. But she refused my pleas to visit. She wouldn't even talk to me. Instead, she had her secretary respond to my many requests without giving a reason for her denial.

The killer decided to plead guilty if his offer of a plea deal was accepted. Part of the condition was that the prison expedited his transfer to a State Correctional Institution. My first memoir, *Gone in an Instant*, shares that story. The sentence was thirty to sixty years for third-degree murder, robbery, carrying an unlicensed firearm and a controlled substance, with intent to deliver and sell the heroin. Tyrone also admitted guilt for buying drugs from Cambria County Drug Task Force confidential informants and trying to get his girlfriend to send him synthetic pot while in prison. That happened a few weeks before Christmas, and my nerves were in tatters. Anger consumed me as time was running out for my visit. It shouldn't have been the DA's decision. If she were in my shoes, I think she would have talked to her child's killer. The only option I had left was to ask the captain to pass on my contact information to Tyrone so that he could try to add me to his visitor list wherever he was sent after the plea deal was accepted. I prayed the captain did as I had asked.

After the sentencing in December 2020, I immediately sent a letter to Tyrone since the prison quickly transferred him to SCI Benner Township in my home state of Pennsylvania. He didn't call or reply to my letter even though I'd provided all my contact information. Years later, I received a text from Vinelink, which is how the Department of Homeland Security updates victims about a prisoner's status. Tyrone had been moved to SCI Camp Hill. Since my aunt lived there, I knew the area well. My letter that day reminded him I'd already forgiven him for Luke's murder, and I prayed for God to open the doors.

Two weeks later, my phone rang. There was no caller ID, but I answered anyway.

"Miss Tammy?"

"Yes."

"This is Tyrone." His voice was deep, and my hand shook as I tried not to drop the phone. *Was this actually my son's killer?*

"What?" I was in shock.

"This is Tyrone," he repeated.

"Oh my! I've been waiting so long to talk to you! How are you? Did you get my letter? I see you've been moved to a new prison."

"Yes. I got your letter. I'll add you to the visitor list and call when it's done."

Tears poured like a faucet. "I don't know if they'll let you see me because they think I'm a victim. Victims aren't allowed to visit."

"I can arrange the visit and will be in touch in a few days."

"OK. I'll visit you as soon as you call because I'm leaving the country for a month-long vacation in two weeks."

We said goodbye and hung up. The call only lasted four minutes. I ran to the kitchen.

My husband turned at the commotion as I entered the room. "Guess who called me?"

"Who?"

"Tyrone! He's going to add me to his visitor list."

Mike, my husband of nineteen years, didn't look thrilled, and I knew he'd rather I not visit a murderer. "Wow. OK."

"Am I allowed to visit him?" Since I'm a Christian and my mom brought me up Presbyterian, God says the husband is the boss unless he tells me to sin.

Mike hugged me. "Sure. I know what this means to you." I kissed him and danced out of the room, wiping away my tears from the fear that he'd say no. God had answered my prayers. But I still prayed that I'd be permitted onto the list, knowing I was a victim. The visit was our secret because I feared someone would call the prison and try to stop it.

Days turned into two weeks, and I lost hope. *I'm a victim, and he's probably unable to add me. Please, God, at least let him call me and let me know.*

I really wanted to see Tyrone before my vacation. How would I relax on our trip after waiting so long to see him? But it wasn't to be.

Mike came home from work on Friday at 4:20 p.m. The weather forecast called for rain, sleet, freezing rain, and high winds; the storm had already begun. We were concerned since the news had reported several fallen trees were causing road closures, so we left quickly. Mike considered putting a Sawzall in the trunk since we would drive on windy mountain country roads for over an hour until we hit the highway. Unfortunately, my mom texted to tell us the power went out shortly after we had left home. And it stayed out until the next day. With the frigid temperatures and no heat, Mike and I were glad we had left when we did.

Dad told us the next day that he'd been out in the storm and barely made it home because every road he tried to take was closed because of downed power lines or trees. I'm glad he was OK and didn't have to sleep the night in his truck. One of these days, he will learn to stay home when it's unsafe.

·♥·♥·♥·♥·♥·

My Transformational Journey

Learning to surrender my emotions to things out of my control was essential to finding peace. Had I trusted God to arrange the visit, I could have enjoyed my vacation with Mike. After all, God was the one who initiated the call from Tyrone in the first place, so if I was meant to see him, God could most certainly make it happen. So why did I doubt the all-powerful, all-knowing, omnipotent God?

10. A Victim, a Killer, and No Bars

On vacation, my phone rang. The caller ID said Orlando, FL. Even though I got numerous daily calls from that area and thought it was another time-share telemarketer, I answered.

"Miss Tammy, it's Tyrone. You're on the list."

My hand shook, and I almost dropped my phone. "That's great news. I'm so excited. I can't wait to see you."

"When can you visit? We can do a video call, or you can come here."

"Oh, no video calls. I want to see you, so I'll come to the prison."

One study revealed that regardless of the length of their incarceration, most prisoners receive only two visits from friends or loved ones during their time behind bars. "Great. I can't wait to see you." He quickly told me how to schedule the visit and instructed me what to wear, or should I say, what *not* to wear.

"Just so you know, I'm out of the country on vacation, so I won't be able to visit for three weeks."

The call only lasted a minute, and as I hung up, happy tears poured onto my chin. Wi-Fi calling was the only way to receive calls since I was in Aruba, and I didn't want to pay for a phone plan. So I was grateful that God ensured I had a signal, so I didn't miss that important call—the call I'd waited almost six years for.

You may wonder why I was happy about meeting Tyrone since I didn't have a typical response. But I don't serve a typical God. The answer is twofold: first, it's God's nature to love, and his Holy Spirit lives in me because I am a child of the most high God. That makes it my nature to love unconditionally.

Let me explain what unconditional love is so you understand. Unconditional love means I love simply because Tyrone is himself, and I don't expect anything in return, just like God loves me unconditionally and expects nothing from me. There are no strings. It has nothing to do with deserving—it is through the grace of God. God demonstrates this kind of love to us and wants us to share it with others.

God doesn't care about Tyrone's past. And I am required to do the same. Luke 15 shares the story of the prodigal son, and those principles apply to Tyrone and me. God loves me unconditionally, and he loves me the same, always and forever. Tyrone doesn't have to measure up to deserve my love. God instructs, teaches, and enables me to receive his love and give this love to others.

Second, Tyrone is my last connection to Luke. He was the last person to be with my son. When my son died, I was still concerned that he wouldn't end up in heaven. God calls us to go into all nations and to make disciples. My job is to be a missionary, sharing the gospel with Tyrone and others in the prison, even the guards.

If I murdered someone, God would still love me since his love is unconditional. I have to do the same. Since Luke died, my spiritual growth has been hard to explain. But sharing my story of salvation with Tyrone so that he could come to know and love God the way I do is part of my stewardship as a Christian. And I am not alone. If you want to read about others who have forgiven those that murdered their family members, Corrie ten Boom forgave the horrible Ravensbruck guard who tortured her at the Nazi concentration camp where her sister Betsie died. Speaker and author Elisabeth Elliot was another missionary who shared Jesus' offer of salvation for two years to the Auca tribe members who killed her husband. So, yes, I was excited to meet Tyrone and complete my God-given missionary work.

Over the next several days, Tyrone's calls blew up my phone. He called at least twice a day. I didn't have a signal for any calls, so I worried something was wrong when I saw all the missed calls every night when I finally had Wi-Fi.

Unfortunately, I had no way of contacting him, so I had to be patient and hope he reached me soon.

The day my husband and I toured the island in a rental car, it surprised me to see that Tyrone had called six times. Yes, six times. *What's going on?* Even Mike became concerned.

One night, after we'd just fallen asleep, my phone rang, causing us both to jump a mile high. I quickly grabbed the phone when I figured it was Tyrone since it was from a 717 area code. It was a different number from the other two calls. A recording said this was a free twenty-second call and that I would need to set up an account and add money if I wanted to talk longer. Then the recording disconnected, and Tyrone was on the line.

"Tammy? It's Tyrone. I need to talk to you!" He sounded desperate. "You've been weighing on my heart. Are you coming to visit, or do you want me to write you a letter to tell you what I must say?"

"I'm out of the country, so I won't be there until the last week of March." Was he finally going to tell me why Luke died? I turned on the light as I sat up in bed.

"Are you going to set up a video call?"

"No. I need to see you in person—I'll come to the prison."

Mike stared at me as I leaned back against the headboard.

"Make sure you don't use drugs twenty-four hours before your visit."

Does Tyrone think I use drugs? "I don't use drugs, so it's fine." What was he thinking? I guess he didn't know me, and my son used marijuana, so maybe he thought I did too.

"Have a blessed night, Tammy." Then I heard a recording saying time was up.

Mike was now sitting up in bed. "I wonder what that was about. Something's up. Did you hear him say 'blessed'?"

"Yes, I did, Mike. I wonder if he's stalking me on social media since people don't talk like that. You know I always say that. I never say 'Happy birthday'; I always say 'Have a blessed birthday'. So something weird is going on."

"I agree. Do prisoners have access to social media?"

"I have no idea."

My heart pounded from that disturbing call, and I stayed awake for the next two hours. While Mike snored beside me, I set up an account through Securus Technologies on my laptop so we could talk longer the next time Tyrone called.

Then I went to the website to set up an account to schedule my prison visit. It was pretty straightforward, but I read the brief rules about passing through security.

·♥·♥·♥·♥·♥·

The following Saturday, we had Wi-Fi for the four hours we spent at the airport. But after our long flight, it surprised me that Tyrone had called an additional six times. *Why didn't my phone ring at the airport?* We wouldn't be home until early Sunday morning, and I planned to drive to my aunt's that afternoon since I'd planned to spend the night with her and her husband. I wanted to know if Tyrone was calling to cancel before my drive. *Please, God, let him call me again before I drive to Carlisle.* My phone finally rang at 3:30 p.m. I was glad I'd held off leaving as long as I could.

"Hey, Tammy, it's Tyrone. Are you still coming to visit? I really need to talk to you."

"Yes. And I added money so we can talk longer than twenty seconds. My visit is scheduled for tomorrow morning at eight-thirty. Didn't anyone tell you? I called the prison, and they said you'd get a notification the day before."

"Yeah. They don't tell us until the evening before."

"Oh. OK. Well, is everything still good for me to visit?"

"Yes. How long can you stay?"

I assumed he didn't know because he didn't have many visitors. "The standard schedule is for three hours. I can stay until eleven-thirty." Mike walked into the bedroom since he'd overheard me on the phone—I always used my speakerphone when I wasn't in public.

"Tammy, can I ask you a few questions?"

"Sure. What's up?"

"How do you feel as a mother who has lost her son?"

Taking a deep breath, I leaned back in my chair as I struggled with how I should answer his question.

"I'm doing well. Just so you know, I'm not angry with you, but I miss Luke terribly. I've forgiven you. You know that."

There was silence on the line. Had Tyrone hung up?

Finally, I heard him clear his throat. "I do."

"Anger will eat you alive. I'm very blessed that God has removed that anger from the moment my son left this earth. You wouldn't even care if I was angry with you, so the only person it would hurt would be me. Know that God will forgive you if you ask him."

"You know I didn't mean to kill him. The gun wasn't supposed to go off. I'm so sorry."

"I'll be there tomorrow morning, and we can talk."

·♥·♥·♥·♥·♥·

Rock music blasted in the car as I sang terribly on the drive to my aunt's. I bellowed along with the music, trying to drown out the pounding of my heartbeat on my two-hour drive the night before my prison visit. *God, please get me there safely*, I prayed as I swerved off the road several times.

At my aunt's, I was so nervous that I barely slept that night, even though the mattress was super soft. The next morning, I drank a cup of Tulsi tea and ate a can of potato soup, hoping the potatoes would put my stomach butterflies to sleep. I used makeup to cover the puffiness under my eyes and drove a mere twenty minutes to SCI Camp Hill.

·♥·♥·♥·♥·♥·

My Transformational Journey

I should have put a lot more thought into my visit with Tyrone. He could have said anything to me. What if he had told me something terrible about Luke and broke my heart? All my cherished memories of my son could have been tainted in three hours. Criminals aren't meant to be trusted. They are in prison for a reason and have been convicted by a judge or jury. I risked eventually having peace by going to the prison, hoping to find that very thing—peace. There is usually a reason when someone is desperate to talk to someone. I should have guarded my heart more and tried to think with my brain instead of my emotions. Caring too much is probably my biggest weakness.

11. A Visit Deep inside a Prison

I'd never been inside a prison before, but when I saw the high black security fence spanning the perimeter of many acres, I knew I was in the right place. Trying to imagine what it would be like if my son was alive and locked in there where I couldn't see him every day, I shed a few tears for Tyrone's parents for the pain they must feel. The emptiness in their hearts knowing that their son was so close, yet so far away. Since I can't visit heaven, I know that feeling too well. But at least they could receive calls and occasionally see their beloved.

Glad I'd arrived ten minutes early—even though I got lost a few times, which shouldn't have happened, as there were only two turns—the extra time allowed me to pray and practice deep breathing to calm my frazzled nerves about what I would soon experience. Seeing Tyrone didn't make me nervous; that excited me. But I was worried about all the strict prison rules I needed to follow, and in the back of my mind, I was worried the powers that be would turn me away since I was a victim.

Mentally, I reviewed the instructions from the prison website I'd read the day before.

Long sleeve shirts only. No hoodies. No showing skin. No cell phones and only your ID and money for the vending machines were allowed inside the visiting area. Check, check, and check. I was good.

A municipal truck almost hit my car as I backed into a parking space in the busy lot. No patience. Grabbing my baggie with my license, four five-dollar bills—the largest amount permitted—and my keys, I stared at several guard towers high above the fence line. Searching for the entrance, I walked through the many parking lots in front of the orangish-red brick complexes. It was eerily quiet as I stared at the sky, wondering if God was still with me. Deep inside, I knew he was.

After several minutes of wandering around in the blustery air, I saw a lady getting out of her truck next to the front of the three-story building that faced the road. That building didn't have a fence around it, so I knew it wasn't the building I needed. The lady didn't look too happy to be there and said she was an employee. She escorted me to the visitors' entrance in a taller building behind the first structure. I was so nervous I couldn't think, and I can't remember much else. I inhaled her unmistakable scent—the same soft, powdery, floral-smelling Baby Soft perfume that my mom wore when I was a child and that put my nerves instantly at ease, taking me back to my childhood—just what I needed.

After hitting the buzzer beside the silver metal door, I heard a click. I rushed to open it, but it was still locked. So I hit the buzzer again, and this time, I was ready as I tugged hard on the heavy door to get it open. An officer in a dark blue uniform sitting behind a barred window greeted me by staring at me. There was no "Hello," no nothing. He wore a name tag, but I couldn't see it without my glasses.

"I'm here to visit Tyrone McDuffie."

"Give me your ID." His no-nonsense voice scared me.

My hand shook as I pulled my driver's license out of a clear plastic Zip-lock baggy and slid it through the tight vertical bars.

He looked at it and then slapped it on the counter in front of me. "Do you have money?"

"Yes."

He pointed to a machine at the back of the starkly plain room. "Get a card from that machine if you plan on using the vending machines. The prison doesn't permit money in the visiting room." That confused me since the website had said I was allowed cash. After using the provided locker key, I left some money and my car keys secured safely.

My nerves caused me to trip over my sneakers as I walked across the white-tiled floor. Staring at the machine, I was ready to scream because it wouldn't take my five-dollar bill. I tried each of my three bills to no avail. Choking back a sob, I used the restroom next to the machine. My head fell into my hands as I sat on the toilet in one of the two stalls and fought back the tears. *Is this a mistake? Am I strong enough to get through this?* I knew I desperately wanted to see Tyrone, but at what cost? I knew all this stress wasn't good for my health, but it had been almost six years since my son's murder, and this twenty-eight-year-old man could tell me why my son had to die. After all, he pulled the trigger from point-blank range. *OK, Tammy. Get it together. You don't have a choice. You know you want to do this. You can do this.*

When I exited the bathroom, I noticed another visitor had arrived. "Can you please help me with the machine?"

She shuffled over to the machine and inserted my money, only to have it spit back out. She tried another dollar. "It isn't working." Then she hit a button and tried again, and magically, out popped a card. She returned to her seat.

I put $5 in two more times, strutted over, and sat beside her, showing her my three cards. She gave me a strange look.

"What's wrong?"

"Oh, no. Come here." She grabbed my cards, and I followed her to the machine, where she inserted each of my cards one after the other.

To my shock, there was only $3.75 on each card.

"They charge a fee for each card."

I'd messed up. Big time. That wouldn't even buy a sandwich; I only had one bill left in the locker.

After retrieving my money from the locker, I added it to one card, giving me $8.75 on that card and $3.75 on the other two. Deflated, I sat back down, ready to cry. Again. The room was perfectly quiet other than my breathing and heart pounding.

I didn't know it then, but God was answering the prayer requests I'd submitted to our church a week prior for him to send people to help me get into the prison without too much difficulty. Many people prayed for me at that exact moment and throughout my visit. I had no idea, and were it not for God's intervention by sending these kind people to help, the visit would have never happened.

Looking at the lady, I figured she wouldn't mind answering more of my questions. "Are the visits in person, or will we be separated by glass?"

"It depends on the crime."

"Our visit is for three hours. I read online that we're allowed a quick hug and kiss at the beginning and end."

"Oh. Then there won't be any glass between you. You can hold hands during the entire visit too."

"Wow. OK. You've been very helpful. Thanks for being kind to a newbie." I smiled at her.

Another woman walked past me carrying a paper. "Is that your paper on the check-in desk?" she asked me.

Quickly, I went to look at the paper, and sure enough, it had Tyrone's name on it, so I knew it was mine. But I didn't realize I was supposed to pick it up. Mr. No Hello man said nothing. *Are any of the employees going to help me?* I'm not a criminal, yet I felt like one.

After grabbing my paper, I turned around, and the lady stared at me. "Did you scrub your hands?"

"No, why?"

"You need to because you've touched money. The guard will test you." I remembered reading that I had two chances to get through security, and if I didn't pass the metal detectors, I had to wait until the end of the line for my third and final try. If I failed, I was out.

After setting my paper on the money machine and putting my locker key in my pocket, I returned to the bathroom. While I was washing, the second lady opened the door. "Scrub. Hard. Get under your nails and don't forget your wrists."

"Ugh. OK." I continued to scrub until my hands were red.

"Rub your skin until it's raw. I'll hold the door for you. Touch nothing."

Wow! I'd never have seen my son's killer if God hadn't put these angels there to help me. I'm glad he was with me. After I exited the bathroom, I grabbed my paper and locker key just as a uniformed guard called me to security.

"Wait, I think you have my key." The second lady ran up to me.

Reaching into my pocket, I pulled out two locker keys. Unfortunately, I also had her paper, not mine. This visit was turning into a nightmare. I handed her the paper and key I'd accidentally taken. Then the guard motioned for me to step forward. "Hands out." He swabbed both my shaking hands, front and back, and rubbed my wrists with an ion wand (Electronic Drug Detection Equipment) that was read by a machine that displayed if there was any trace amount of illegal substances found. Whew! I passed. A quick internet search shows that four out of five bills have been in contact with cocaine, and there is a very high chance that an ion scanner will test positive even after thorough hand washing. I'm glad I wasn't in that 80 percent. Some guards may test your clothes, shoes, pockets, and license, so I hoped I got in next time and wasn't one of the unfortunate ones with a false positive since I don't nor have I ever used illegal drugs.

I turned to walk through the metal detector. "Wait. Hold up. Is that a hoodie?" My shirt had a thick collar because I was always cold, but I showed him it didn't have a hood. The guard motioned for me to proceed.

I bounced through the metal detector since I hadn't risked wearing any jewelry.

A guard buzzed me through the next door in the back of the building, where I entered a short, empty hall. The first door closed before a buzz sounded for me to go through a second heavy metal door. It was a little nerve-wracking for the few seconds when I was locked between doors, and I can't imagine the life a prisoner faces every day. Then I was outside in the high-wired fenced area. I followed the long, lonely sidewalk down the hill to the building on the left, walking quickly since all this took precious time away from my limited visit. The next building was taller, with many windows above the first floor. There were probably bars on them, but my mind wasn't 100 percent clear. As soon as the buzzer sounded, my sweaty palm pulled the door handle to enter, and I walked straight to the end of the long hall.

·♥·♥·♥·♥·♥·

My Transformational Journey

I'm a stickler for doing research before everything I do, whether it's a trip or buying a car. So why didn't I research more about what was involved in entering a prison? Websites about that prison would have helped me find out where the visitor center was, and I would have been more relaxed. Instead, I let my nerves take over, overruling any common sense I had. But God had everything under his control—I just didn't know it then.

12. Prison Looked like a Place for Children

There were vibrant yellow and blue Minions painted on both walls, and I found that interesting. Other cartoons were also painted on the walls, but I only remember the Minions as I thought about how the art would delight young visitors. Tyrone greeted me when I entered the room at the end of the very long hall. He wore an orange jumpsuit with beige on the bottom of the sleeves, thick socks over his calves, and slip-on beige shoes. My heart pounded as my nervousness caused me to sweat when I saw Tyrone smile at me.

"Miss Tammy, I apologize for my looks and wish I would've cleaned up for you." He tried to smooth his frizzy, wild, black hair, which stuck out several inches from his head—I'm sure it was hard to manage since grooming products were expensive in prison. His body towered over me as he hugged me quickly. "I'm excited and nervous to meet you."

Probably almost as excited as I was to see him.

"Where do you want to sit?" He indicated the seats on the right side of the large room where three other visitors were already sitting with their incarcerated loved ones.

"Let's sit in the back by the block wall." As we walked, I looked at the water pouring from the ceiling out of the huge pipes. And more pipes were bursting by the second. The prison had severe leaks, and I had no idea what was causing the cracks.

We sat against the wall, and he immediately stood back up. "It smells like ass in here. We're under a cell block."

"I don't smell anything." Standing up, I followed him as he walked toward another area of seats.

Looking around, I saw other leaks starting—I'm not talking about a trickle. Water was pouring from the pipes, hard enough to fill a large swimming pool in a matter of hours. The rushing water was so loud that I barely heard the guard's announcement. "Get what you want from the vending machines before we get evacuated."

Oh no, is our visit getting canceled? As I walked toward the vending machines, a strong smell overwhelmed me. Gagging, I pushed it to the back of my mind.

Tyrone was across the room. I waved to get his attention. "Tyrone, what do you want to eat and drink? I don't know what you like." That was only the third time I'd seen him, and the first two were in court, so we'd never talked much, let alone discussed his taste in food.

"Anything but pork."

OK. That didn't help me much. Couldn't he have been a little more specific? I stared at the food choices and thought about how blessed I was. It was a miracle I could even visit.

All the other visitors were already making their purchases. There were several hoagies to choose from, and I felt overwhelmed. *How had I thought I could handle this?* I wasn't mad in the least that he killed my son. I'd completely forgiven him, and since it's my nature to be a people-pleaser, I wanted to make him happy. So I chose the sub that was twice as big as the others. After inserting my card, I asked the lady I'd met previously, "What do I do now?"

"Hit the letter and number for your selection."

Imagine that? It was just like every other vending machine I had ever used, except I couldn't use this one. The Italian sandwich didn't drop—it just slid forward, camping on the edge.

A nearby guard walked up to me. "What happened?"

"I didn't get my selection?" A tear slid down my cheek as I panicked. My money was gone because the sandwich didn't drop, and I only had enough money on the other cards to buy a few soda bottles. *I'm so stupid.*

The guard pressed a few buttons, popped my card out, and put it back in. "Pick something. Quick. That one didn't work because it was too far back."

"I can get it now since it's on the edge."

"No! Pick something else and hurry."

"But I don't know what Tyrone likes." More tears filled my eyes.

"Get the turkey sandwich. Hit A2."

The sandwich fell to the bottom, and I lifted the lid while everyone else left the room except the security man, the guard, and Tyrone.

The guard grabbed a plate and napkins. Grabbing the sandwich from my hand, he threw it on the plate. "Grab condiments!" The noise got louder as the water poured next to us, and it was getting louder by the minute.

I stood there shaking. Dumbfounded. He threw mustard, mayonnaise, ketchup, salt, and pepper packets onto the plate with the submarine.

"Get a soda."

"I don't know what he drinks."

"Honey, he hasn't had soda in years. He'll like whatever you get him." I was alone as he walked away.

I grabbed two Sprites and walked to the guard, handing him my card. "Here, you can have this since there's only seventy-five cents left on it."

He returned it to me. "Keep it. You can put more money on it next time."

Why am I so stupid? Is it just my nerves from this visit? I was surprised I could speak and walk since I couldn't seem to do anything else. That was three angels God had sent to help me. How many more would I need to get through this visit?

"Just so you know, no one here will help you." The guard clasped his hands together. "You're on your own. The others aren't like me."

Thank you, God. Wow! You're really taking care of me today. I was so glad many prayer warriors were praying for me at that exact moment.

I returned to the desk at the end of the long hall. I gasped as water started pouring from the enormous pipes above the desk, soaking the security man. The entire room would soon flood at this rate. It did smell like butt. I wondered if it was from sewer pipes. Ew!

·♥·♥·♥·♥·♥·

My Transformational Journey

Society treats you by the friends you keep. Since I rarely judge people and give most people the benefit of the doubt, I never even thought about what the employees at the prison would think of me. If I'd known, I might have been better prepared for what happened. Maybe I would have told them my story.

13. A CRAYON FOR PROTECTION FROM MY SON'S KILLER

Tyrone seemed happy with my choices when I handed him the sub and drink. "I'm sorry if this isn't what you want because I didn't know what you liked."

Unfortunately, a half-hour of our visit was already gone. The guard escorted us to another room back down the Minion-covered hall. After we sat, I asked if I could write notes about the visit since we planned to discuss the night of Luke's murder. I was sure my husband and family would want to know what Tyrone had to say, and since I've had PTSD and COVID since that traumatic event, I struggled to remember information. So Tyrone volunteered to ask the guard to give him paper and a crayon—I was later told the Crayola was for everyone's safety.

Looking around the room, I noticed tiny windows near the ceiling in the block walls. There were two restrooms at one end next to more vending machines, which appeared primarily empty, besides a few soda bottles. But what was important was that there were no leaking pipes, and flooding didn't cut my visit short. Soft rock music from the eighties played from an overhead speaker, and visitors were far enough apart that conversations were private. Tyrone and I sat at the very back of the room, where we had the most privacy. The lady who had helped me with the card machine had her arms wrapped around a man the entire visit—I'm guessing it was her husband. The other two visitors held hands with their significant others, but Tyrone and I sat side by side with a small table between us. It was a seat I'd intentionally chosen.

I thought about the shooting. Jayme had driven Luke to Old Cone-maugh that night, so I knew Luke had $1,200 on him to buy a gun. My son was paranoid and thought a gun would make him feel safe. While I disagreed with Luke's decision to buy a gun, I still don't feel he should have died because he had $1,200 on him, but God controlled everything and had allowed my son to pass on.

Tyrone took a big gulp of Sprite. "On the streets, they called me T-wa. Before Luke died, I'd met Drew (Andrew) in a nearby convenience store a few days earlier. I could immediately tell he was a junkie, so I gave him my number. He called twenty minutes later."

"T-wa, can you hook me up?"

"Who's this?"

"I just met you a few minutes ago at the store. You gave me your number."

"Yeah. I remember."

"Can we try your product?"

"Sure. What's the address? I'll be right over."

Tyrone said he followed Drew's directions and took both of his prod-ucts to the house. He found Nick there with Andrew. After the two of them tried the products, they made a small purchase. Tyrone asked if he could sit on the floor to roll a joint since there wasn't any furniture in the living room other than a bed. When he used his knees as a table, he said his personal protection was poking him, so he set the gun next to him on the floor.

I took a drink of soda so Tyrone wouldn't see my reaction. "What happened next?"

"The next day, Drew called and said they wanted to buy more dope. A lot more. They barred the door and wouldn't let me in when I got to the house. Drew said we needed to do the deal outside—that made me nervous. They came out the door, and a minute later, someone else came out of the house. He was clean-shaven, and I could tell this kid had never touched dope in his life. I could see his arms below his white T-shirt, which were clean—there were no track marks."

"That was Luke."

"You know the rules I set when we met yesterday," Tyrone told Nick and Andrew. "No one else is to be around. So why'd you call me? And who's this kid?"

Tyrone told me Nick said that Luke was a trustworthy friend. All four walked up the alley, and Tyrone tried to separate from them. "Get away from me; I want nothing to do with this." Yet I discovered in Tyrone's subsequent statement that Luke was still walking beside him. Why, I will never know. If Tyrone wanted to escape them and was unnerved about not being let in the house, why was he willingly walking next to a stranger?

"When Luke reached into his backpack, I panicked and grabbed his hand. I thought he was trying to rob me. We struggled. When Luke grabbed me with his other hand, I used my free hand to pull my gun. It went off. I didn't mean to shoot him. I grabbed his backpack and walked off, passing a camera as I went by."

That didn't make any sense to me. If the gun went off accidentally, how had Tyrone shot a bullet precisely into Luke's head, which caused him to die instantly? That would have been hard to do by accident.

"Why was Luke next to you if you were trying to escape them?" He either didn't answer or said something that made little sense because I don't remember his answer. It must have been inconsequential. "Tyrone, what was in Luke's backpack?"

"There was a baggie of brownies and a few capsules."

"The brownies were marijuana brownies, and the capsules were THC oil extracted from the marijuana."

"That's interesting, but I didn't know that then."

Loud voices disturbed our conversation as the two guards in the front of the room passed the time.

"Tyrone, can I ask you something?

"Sure."

"Did Luke's death have anything to do with a gang initiation?"

"No, it didn't." He took a breath and appeared to be deep in thought. "Did you know you can get drugs in prison?"

I looked around the room. It would have been hard for someone to sneak drugs in with all the security I went through.

"No. I mean, maybe I'd heard about it—making wine from fruit in toilets or something."

"I stay away from drugs, and I'm concentrating on my future."

He appeared sincere, and I hoped he was. But why had he brought up a conversation about drugs in the prison?

"What happened after you left my son?"

"My cousin heard on the scanner that the police were looking for me, so he split."

"Was your cousin the man in the news video the police were searching for?" A few days after Luke's shooting, the local news and newspaper shared a screenshot from a video of Tyrone and another man. The blurry image showed the men wearing matching white shirts with black stripes on the shoulders and black Nike shorts, but their faces were unrecognizable.

"Yes. But he had nothing to do with it." After slathering several packets of mayonnaise and salt and pepper on his turkey sandwich, Tyrone took a bite.

"You know, Tyrone, Luke had $1,200 on him. He was there to buy a gun—from you."

"That's crazy. Guns on the street don't cost that much. They sell for $150. Everyone knows that."

"Well, my son didn't."

Tyrone swallowed another bite without chewing. I thought back to a video of Tyrone, which was all over the internet right after the shooting. In it, he was banging on the doors of several homes, asking where his gun was. And by asking, I mean yelling. The cops never elaborated, but I still wonder about it. If Tyrone was looking for his gun, maybe it was premeditated murder. But I couldn't go there. Murder was one thing. But premeditation was another.

Tyrone interrupted those thoughts. "Twelve hundred dollars will get you an AK-47. And if he had that much money, he wasn't there to rob me. Anyone with that kind of money doesn't need to do that."

"Tyrone, something is missing from this story."

"I now believe your son wasn't trying to rob me. If only I could go back and let it play out, he'd still be alive. I'm sorry."

That didn't make sense. I'd had high hopes of hearing the truth because I was an optimist.

"You know, I saw Drew while I was still at the Cambria County Prison. He was in another cell block, but I tapped on the connecting wall."

"Really? I knew he spent a few months there, but I never knew Andrew talked to you."

"Yeah. He did."

That was interesting. After Tyrone shot Luke, Nick and Andrew ran off, terrified. Then they called 911. Why would Andrew talk to Tyrone if he was so afraid of him?

"Also, I should've got a lighter sentence. My first attorney quit the case, which looked bad because it made me look guilty."

I wish I'd thought to ask why his attorney dropped the case. *Did the money run out, so public defenders took over the case?*

"Tyrone, I didn't go to that hearing because the first time I saw you, you sat in the front of the courtroom with your attorney, whom you'd just met, and you kept looking back at me, laughing. That upset me very much because my son was dead because of you, and you dared to look at me and laugh."

"I'm sorry. So sorry. Miss Tammy, let me tell you what happened. My dad hired Tariq Shabazz, an attorney from Philadelphia. He was a tall, bald, black man, and he was telling me how everyone was joking about who he was there to represent."

I didn't get the joke, so I kept my mouth shut.

"Well, Tyrone, that upset me. So bad that I felt the need to leave the country so that I couldn't be at the next hearing. I felt I owed it to Luke to support his case, but I couldn't. And it's a good thing I didn't because the video of the shooting would've killed me. And also, my family said your attorney was waving around the autopsy photos so everyone in the room could see them. That would've been my undoing since I was already suicidal."

"I'm sorry I killed him, but I'm the 'effect' that killed him," he said. "I'm not the cause. Others put me in this situation, and I regret the outcome. My dad paid Tariq $10,000 to represent me, and Tariq hired a private investigator with $2,000 of that money. I have over 1,200 pages I'd like to send you about the case; I'll send them in two weeks when I've got more money in my account because I need to pay for copies, envelopes, and postage."

That day had not turned out as I had expected. Nothing made sense. He didn't provide any answers. I can't even tell you why I didn't have the courage to ask the questions that lay on my heart: why was he so desperately banging on doors looking for a gun only a few hours before the murder? If it was an accident, how did the gun go off precisely on Luke's head, instantly killing him?

·♥·♥·♥·♥·♥·

My Transformational Journey

Pay attention to what people tell you, especially the man who murdered your son. Why did he give me so many irrelevant details? Was he just glad to have company and someone to talk to? Or was he trying to manipulate me? The PI report intrigued me, and I wanted to read it. But, yet again, it would be wise for me to remember that the PI was working for Tyrone, so that information was biased.

14. Spending Three Hours with a Killer

"OK. Can I ask you something?" I picked up my crayon to take more notes. "Why did you say 'Have a blessed night' to me on the phone? No one talks like that. Have you looked at my social media?"

"Not since last year when my friend looked you up. But I said that because my grandma always said that."

"She used the word *blessed* all the time?"

"Yes. Grandma took me to church for the first eleven years of my life."

"That's interesting."

I wrote with the blue crayon on my paper because I didn't want to forget about his wonderful grandma.

"You know I'm studying to go into real estate development when I leave here. I'll be fifty-two then."

"That's great. You know I have an escrowed real estate license." I looked around for a clock since I hadn't been permitted to wear my Apple watch. "And I'm fifty-two now."

"Do you have any rentals?"

"Yes. We still have five apartments, but we've sold the rest. I don't like it. Some tenants can be a pain to deal with."

Someone exited the bathroom and slammed the door, drawing my attention away from Tyrone. That's when I saw a photo machine. *I wonder if I can get a picture of us.* That was a weird thought, but I wanted one—I can't explain why.

"Did Luke go to college?"

"No. My son hated school."

"I loved school. I took a few college courses; my favorite subjects were reading and math. I read lots of books. Right now, I'm reading about body language. It's really interesting." Tyrone looked at the crayon still in my hand.

"Did you know I wrote a book?"

Tyrone smiled widely. I wondered why that excited him.

"No. What's it about?"

"My son's murder. It's a memoir." My fingers tightly gripped the crayon as I thought about my life without Luke.

"What's it called? I'll see if I can find it in our eBook library. I'd love to read it."

"*Gone in an Instant: Losing My Son. Loving His Killer.* By me, of course."

Tyrone's mouth fell open. He didn't say anything for at least a minute.

"You're kidding?"

"No. I'm serious."

"I have to read that. Is it on Amazon?"

"Yes."

"Can you send me a copy?"

"Yes. I can do that."

"Have Amazon ship it to the Bellefonte office, and they'll inspect it and give it to me. Of course, you can't send anything directly."

"I'll order it as soon as I get home."

Reading my book may change his life. Is this a good idea? Will he hate me after he reads it? Maybe I shouldn't have offered to send him a copy.

"My sister loves to read, so I'll tell her about it, and she and my dad can share it on their social media."

"That sounds good." After picking up my paper from the table, I stared at my notes. Tyrone shocked me with what he said next.

"Maybe we can write a book together."

"That would be hard. And books aren't cheap. *Gone in an Instant* cost me over $10,000 to pay for editors, covers, proofreaders, an audiobook, etc., and it takes a lot of time." My head spun, thinking about the possibilities. Maybe we could go on tour and share how people must forgive to overcome their grief.

"You know, Tyrone, one day, after I'd sent that first letter, I received a call from prison. It was from someone named Tyrone. But when I answered, he said he was trying to reach someone in Alabama and had the wrong number."

"That was me." He laughed. His laugh was beautiful, and I'm sure he probably didn't have much to laugh about being locked up. "What are the chances that you'd get a call from prison from someone named Tyrone?"

"Why didn't you talk to me?"

"I was scared—I killed your son."

The remaining time flew by. When I looked up, I realized we were the last ones in the room. I'd just spent three hours with my son's killer and had enjoyed it. The stern-looking guard signaled for us to vacate the room with a wave of his hand.

I hugged Tyrone. "I'll put money on your commissary so you can send me letters and mail copies from the PI."

Before I walked out, Tyrone pointed to a phone number he'd written on my paper with the crayon. "Can you call my dad and wish him a happy birthday from me? His birthday is today."

"Sure. I'll do that for you."

The check-out guard was unhappy when I interrupted him. "How do I use the machine to add money to someone's commissary? I need to run to my car to get my credit card."

"The door will lock in ten minutes, so hurry."

I ran to my car and sprinted back. It probably took me three minutes. At the door, I heard someone inside say, "There she is."

After I pressed the buzzer, the intercom came on. "Can I help you?"

"I need to put money into the commissary machine."

"We're closed until twelve-fifteen."

My head dropped, and I slouched as I walked away, contemplating what to do. I'd have saved money by putting it on the machine instead of doing it over the internet. Exhausted, I bit the bullet and decided to do it from home, as I still had a long drive ahead of me and was emotionally spent. In my car, I prayed for God to give me safe travels home. It exhilarated me to have finally seen Tyrone after all these years. But I thought about how ironic it was that I went to the prison to get answers and came away with more questions. *Will it ever end? Or should I just let it go?*

It cost me an extra $5 when I finally completed the commissary transaction, plus a $12 cash advance fee from my credit card. Tyrone never asked me for any money. I gave it.

·♥·♥·♥·♥·♥·

My Transformational Journey

Did Tyrone use me to get free money? I'm very gullible, and it would have been better if I had talked to Mike before putting money into Tyrone's account. Since Mike wasn't emotionally involved, he probably could have given me sound advice. Instead, I jumped in with both feet before seeing how deep the water was. I was curious to see what Tyrone thought of my book too. I found the Bellefonte address and sent a copy via Amazon as soon as I could.

15. A Chaplain's Perspective on Inmates and Visitors

As I've learned from experience, there are always reasons for people's actions. The guards had their reasons for treating me the way they did. Don Schreier, a dear friend and mentor, worked in the prison system for years. Don agreed to share details so I could better understand how hard their job was. Thank you, Don. What follows is Don's perspective:

You never forget the first time you enter a prison—it's a very unique experience. Prison's lack of freedom is so foreign to life as most people know it. To work in a prison is a job like no other, as you are locked behind secured doors and fences with a multitude of convicted criminals.

I served as a chaplain for nine years in a state correctional facility. I was a staff member on the "treatment" side of prison operations, while correction officers were on the "security" side of operations. Although both sides worked together, there was constant tension between facilitating treatment for inmates and maintaining security.

Inmates or convicts must learn how to survive in a challenging and harsh environment. To cope, they do what is necessary—some are bullies, others are softies, all create some sort of shell in order to protect themselves until their time is served and they are released. Oftentimes, an inmate "cons" to get by. He will lie to anyone about anything in order to cope. There is little to no trust between inmates and staff.

Inmates came to my office for counsel, help with a problem, or to seek a phone call for a family emergency. Many told me they were innocent of the charges that brought them to prison. My response was always the same: "A judge and jury found you guilty. They had the evidence presented to them; I didn't. Therefore, let's just work from today forward." My goal was to serve and help inmates improve themselves so that when released from prison, if not serving a life sentence, they would be able to cope better and contribute to society. I worked with the psychologist and treatment specialists to help inmates learn to help themselves and fulfill their treatment program. An inmate needed to do at least three things to be considered for parole: 1) admit to the crime they were incarcerated for, 2) stay out of trouble, and 3) fulfill all the requirements of their treatment program (sex offender treatment, anger management, etc.).

Correction officers were tasked with the responsibility of keeping the prison safe and secure for inmates and staff. This was no small task. The prison I worked at had 1,300 inmates from various social backgrounds and religious groups locked behind two high fences lined with concertina wire. Many were from abusive families. Some were on the edge of insanity, and many were violent criminals. Most never learned how to respect authority and follow rules and guidelines. Locking them up together in minimal living conditions was a recipe for trouble.

Correction officers had a challenging and dangerous job; for eight hours a day, they checked into a world like no other. Therefore, in order to cope with the human darkness, evil, and danger of their work environment, they, too, wore a protective shell. They smiled a little depending on the circumstance, but were always vigilant for the possibility of trouble brewing just below the surface of the daily routine. Working in this type of environment for years takes its toll on a person.

When someone enters the prison to visit an inmate, it's just another workday for the correction officer to maintain security and safety. All visitors must follow strict rules to enter the prison; if they don't, they lose their visitation privileges. In some cases, they may even be arrested for trying to sneak in contraband for an inmate. This happens more than you might think. Correction officers working in the visiting room are always vigilant and focused for any kind of illegal or bad behavior.

When Tammy showed up at the prison for her first visit, she simply stepped into a world she had never encountered before. It was all so foreign to her. It was not that the prison staff treated her differently or badly; it was just another day at work for them. Most people working in prisons are good people working in a very harsh environment. Tammy needed to learn prison visitation protocol. She'll never forget her first visit to the state prison.

·♥·♥·♥·♥·♥·

My Transformational Journey

Always trust others and ask for advice when dealing with something you know nothing about. I was grateful to Don for sharing his perspective about what it was like to work in a prison. It sounds like a challenging job where you would constantly need to be on guard to avoid being taken advantage of by a prisoner. Anyone who chooses to work in these positions has my utmost admiration, respect, and gratitude.

16. My Call to a Murderer's Dad

I called Tyrone's dad shortly after I got home. He answered on the second ring.

"Mr. McDuffie?"

"Yes, who's this?" His voice was gruff.

"This is Tammy Horvath, the mother of the kid your son murdered. Tyrone asked me to call you and wish you a happy birthday."

"When did you talk to my son?"

"I spent three hours visiting him today at the prison."

"You did? You're amazing. I can't believe you'd do that. You know Tyrone didn't mean to kill your son? Your son was trying to rob him."

"Well, you need to talk to your son because, after our conversation today, he no longer feels that way."

"Miss Mary. I can't believe you called me to give me a message." His voice broke, and I think he might have been crying.

"It's Tammy." I tried not to cry myself—my heart broke for this father who'd lost his son to a minimum of thirty years in prison.

"I can't believe you visited him. I'm so sorry this happened. We have both lost a child." He sniffled.

"I understand. And I feel your pain. But I don't blame you for any of this."

"You know, my boy called me that night. He said, 'They comin' to get me, Dad. Help me! I don't know what to do. They comin'. Please, Dad. Help!' I didn't know what to do for him. I was hours away, and it was the middle of the night. He said, 'I killed someone.' I said to him, 'Oh, son. What can I do? It's too late.'"

"I can't imagine how you felt. I'm sure your heart was broken."

"It sure was."

"Your son asked me to send him a copy of the book I wrote about my son's murder." I told him the title.

"Can you please send me an autographed copy? Did my son tell you who I am?"

"What do you mean?"

He mumbled something about Biggie Smalls, Puff, and DJ Noodles, but I had trouble understanding him. *What the heck is going on here?*

"I'm an influencer on Social Media." I wasn't sure he was actually an influencer, but I wanted to share the book with him anyway.

I continued to talk because this man seemed heartbroken. "Tyrone said he never received the letter I sent him in 2020. I've been trying that long to get a hold of him."

"I'll tell you the truth—he received the letter. He has it."

"OK. Why did Tyrone tell me he didn't?"

"He couldn't face you after what he did. He feels bad."

That's one lie I'd been told by Tyrone so far. *Who says they didn't receive a letter when they had?*

That was the longest half hour of my life, and I was glad when the call ended. It was hard hearing him apologize many times about my son's murder and hearing that he thought Luke was there to rob Tyrone because I knew he wasn't.

Tyrone called me that night to make sure I'd made it home safely, and I told him I had given his father his message. He was delighted with me.

"Why didn't you call your dad yourself?" He said he didn't have his dad's number. I wondered if all criminals think that no one will catch their lies—he was the one who gave me the number. Maybe it was more that his dad, or Tyrone himself, didn't have money to pay for the call. I thought I was being played, but I didn't know why.

After a good night's sleep, I woke early to mind-buzzing alerts. I realized Tyrone had said during one of our calls that he had replied to my letter via a text message that the prison had arranged. When I'd questioned him about it, he'd said, "About that. I'd asked my friend to message you, and I'm sure he didn't." Lie three. But who was counting?

Also, I didn't believe what Tyrone said about how the murder happened because it made little sense; I was very disappointed. The night Luke died, he was there to buy a gun, and if he had gotten the gun, he would have left. And Luke had a large machete in his backpack that his friend saw on the way to the town, and when I asked Tyrone if it was in the backpack, Tyrone said no. The other thing that made little sense was he said there wasn't any money. Luke had $1,200 on him—Jayme saw it.

So now I had more questions than answers about why Luke had died. But I was OK not knowing if that was God's plan, and I've been OK not knowing. I was hoping God would share the details with me, but he has his reasons for giving me more questions.

None of these details matter as God has already blessed me with peace because I've fully surrendered my will to him. While it would have been nice to hear the truth, it won't change how I feel about Tyrone, and I won't treat him differently because of it. I hoped that him knowing that I'd forgiven him might mean he would come clean about his part in the terrible situation.

I want my life to make a difference—I want to be used by God to help others by being a good steward. God definitely used me to help Tyrone, and I know this because his first words on our first call were, "I'll never forget your Christmas gift to me in court. You said that since Jesus forgave you for your sins, as a Christian, you were to forgive me. And you did. That's the nicest thing anyone has done for me. I've been thinking a lot about that." I wished I'd had a chance to share more of the gospel with Tyrone so he could find the same inner peace I have. But God didn't open that door. Instead, God probably used me to plant a few more seeds.

My life goal is to serve my God-given purpose and help others find the grace Jesus offers everyone when he died on the cross so we can be with him in heaven for eternity. John 3:16 says, "For God so loved the world that he gave his one and only Son, that whoever believes in him shall not perish but have eternal life."

In John 8:12, Jesus says, "I am the light of the world, whoever follows me will never walk in darkness, but will have the light of life."

If you haven't accepted this offer of salvation, will you consider doing it now and make Jesus the Lord of your life? There is a deadline if you want to share in Jesus' light. We only have until our last breath to accept Jesus' generous gift of eternal life offered through grace. Just pray this prayer or use your own words.

A SINNER'S PRAYER:

Dear Jesus, I believe in you. I believe you are the Son of God, that you died for my sins, and that you were buried and rose again as written in the Bible. Please come into my heart so I can have eternal life. Fill me with the Holy Spirit and help me live the way you want me to. Forgive me for my past sins. Guide me in my future so that I can live my life for you. Amen.

The Bible says the only unpardonable sin is not accepting Jesus as your Savior.

·♥·♥·♥·♥·♥·

My Transformational Journey

Just because someone's family member has committed a crime doesn't mean the family doesn't feel any pain. My son was in heaven, but Mr. McDuffie also lost his son. I don't know how old Tyrone's dad is, but because he has cancer, and even if he didn't, he may very well never see his son outside of prison bars again. And he has yet to visit him inside the prison. My heart breaks for him. Most people wouldn't even think about the family who hurt them, but God wired me differently. I wish I could take their pain away, but I can't. It's always important to remember that everyone has feelings. Mine aren't the most important.

17. A WANTED MAN ON THE RUN FROM THE LAW

Before my prison visit, I'd been hanging out with Nick and giving him occasional rides to work. We'd grown close, and he'd learned to trust me when he realized I truly loved him and had his best interests at heart. I shared the gospel about Jesus wanting Nick to become a Christian.

In the months leading up to Luke's murder, Nick had been hooked on heroin. He shared this with me when I unexpectedly surprised him at his dad's house where he lived.

"Nick, I want you to know that I've been to visit Tyrone."

"Really. Wow!"

"Yes. Just last week. Tell me about your arrest. How did you end up in prison?"

"I was on Cambria County's wanted list for fighting and fleeing the state. Having been in prison for two days in the past, I knew what to expect. I didn't want to return, so I ran to Louisiana instead of facing the charges."

"Nick, I'm so sorry."

I squeezed his shoulder to let him know I cared.

"I had to sell platelets at a blood and plasma donation center to afford the bus fare so I could eventually return to Pennsylvania. My pap escorted me to the prison two days later to turn myself in. Pap was afraid I'd run again. The court sentenced me to six months for disorderly conduct."

"I know nothing about prison. Were there women there?"

Nick stooped to pick up a black and white kitten entering the living room.

"They're in a different area. It was rough. I was glad I was only at the county level rather than the state level."

"What was it like? I mean, what happened after you turned yourself in?"

"After giving digital fingerprints and having my picture taken, I had to strip naked and was searched without any contact. Then someone listed my tattoos. After showering, I dressed."

"What clothes did they provide?"

The kitten meowed as Nick held her. "Pale-yellow clothes that resembled scrubs—they were itchy. I kept my sneakers, but they took my shoelaces. When I had enough money, I paid $5 for bright orange Crocs."

"I can't even imagine what that was like. Tell me more."

Nick petted the kitten. She purred as we continued our conversation.

"The prison's a medium security block with an open cell. Six of us shared three sets of bunk beds in a room with no door."

"Was it hard to sleep?"

"The mattress had plastic over thin foam on a metal frame, which was uncomfortable. There were no pillows, and the blanket was itchy wool." Nick looked deep in thought. "And loud snoring at night made it hard to sleep. A separate area in the cell block had a toilet, showers, and a sink."

"Yikes. I can't imagine sleeping in a room full of snoring people. It's hard enough listening to my husband every night." The adorable kitten crawled onto my lap.

"None of my family put money in my commissary, and I was starving. Since I'm great at drawing, other prisoners paid me to draw family portraits or make them birthday cards with the paper and pencils the prison provided. The strap of the Croc made an excellent eraser since the pencils didn't have any. The extra money bought food."

A car door shut; Nick's dad entered the house, and pots clanked in the kitchen.

"Yikes! Not having access to food would've been my undoing, Nick."

My belly rumbled as I thought about someone taking chocolate away from me.

"The food was assigned every day of the week. They valued the meal at $0.37, and the food was bland. Every other Tuesday was tacos; that was the most filling meal. One time, a fight started over a sports game. Two big muscular guys beat the crap out of a man before leaving him lying in a pool of blood. When the guards found him, they took him to the infirmary. Since he was unconscious, they must've played the video because they put the aggressors in the hole."

"That's terrible." Warm sunlight hit me through the window. "Were you able to go outside?"

"Yes. There was an outside recreation area with concrete walls and a fence over the top. There was a basketball hoop, so I played with the others. That was the best thing about prison."

"Thanks for sharing with me." I said goodbye to Nick and the kitten before heading home.

·♥·♥·♥·♥·♥·

Since I'd been sharing the gospel with Nick, I prayed for God to open his heart. One day, while I was giving Nick a ride home, he said, "Luke told me I needed God in my life. He said I needed to pray to ask God into my heart so I don't go to hell when I die. Luke had said pleadingly to me, 'It isn't worth the risk for something as stupid as not praying and asking Jesus to be your Lord and Savior. What do you have to lose?'"

"Wow, Nick. I didn't know my son had done that for you. How do you feel? Is that something you'd like to do—do you want to ask Jesus into your heart and make him your Lord and Savior?"

"Yes, I do." His voice was choked with emotion.

It was raining as I parked in front of Nick's dad's house. I grabbed Nick's hands. "Repeat after me, but only if you mean and agree with my words."

After we finished the prayer, Nick was emotional. We looked into the stormy sky, and rain pounded the car's windshield. The clouds parted, and the sun shone through, casting rays through the window on us. Nick looked up, mesmerized. "I've never experienced anything like that."

"That's God showing you his love." I wrapped Nick in a warm embrace. "I love you, and so does God. Don't ever forget it."

"I won't, and I'm going to read Luke's Bible tonight." Luke had two Bibles when he died, and I'd given Nick one. I knew he treasured it.

The next day, Nick's text said, "This is the first time since I was a kid that I can feel my heart full of hope and peace."

Nick was the second person I'd led to Jesus. My son was the first. I'm usually a seed planter for God's kingdom—meaning I typically share the Good News, but someone else does the salvation prayer. God gave me a magnificent gift by letting me finish something my son had started a month before he died.

I'm so proud of Nick because I know it wasn't easy getting off heroin. I won't go into the details of how he did that because that is his story to tell, but he permitted me to share all of this. So even when life seems dark, and the devil tries his hardest to beat us down, we can take comfort that God loves us and will help us fight our battles. God used Nick's dad, stepmom, and grandparents to help him get the counseling he needed to overcome his demons. Like Tyrone, Nick's gram had taken him to church as a child. I am grateful to these loving grandparents who care enough about their grandchildren's eternal home after their earthly life ends.

·♥·♥·♥·♥·♥·

My Transformational Journey

If I had been in Nick's shoes, would I have been able to turn myself into prison? And if I did, would I have been strong enough to survive? Probably not. Anytime anyone upsets me, I cry. Anytime I'm hurt, I cry. Anytime I feel unloved, I cry. Therefore, I wouldn't survive in prison because you can't show weakness, or people will use that against you. Like the guy lying in his pool of blood, I, too, would've been beaten until I succumbed to whatever the other inmates wanted me to do. It would only take minimal torture to make me cry like a baby.

18. Life Ends for Some but Goes On for Others

Tyrone's grandmother planted a seed of Jesus' love in Tyrone, and I hoped it would grow. The seed is God's Word and sharing the Good News of Jesus' death on the cross, offering salvation to all who accept. Would God allow me to be a part of it? Tyrone was supposed to call after he had received my book. That had been two weeks ago. Another visit to the prison weighed deep on my heart, and I hoped to water the seed. Clicking on the website's page that said I was still an approved visitor, I saw that every date for sixty days said there was no time slot available. That could have been because Tyrone had used his allotted time, gotten into trouble, or some other reason that I'd never know since I was working with a convoluted bureaucracy. My visit wasn't meant to be.

Concern overwhelmed me—my tears poured. Had something happened? Did Tyrone read my book? Had it pushed him over the edge, causing him to take his own life since he'd claimed to have attempted that when he was arrested for Luke's murder? An employee of the prison responded to my email and stated, "He is not currently able to have visits. Once he is, you will be able to schedule." That was it. Hopefully, he was OK.

Tyrone's dad had also had plenty of time to read *Gone in an Instant*, so I called his number, hoping he'd know if his son was alright. A recorded message said, "The subscriber you have dialed is not in service." Mr. McDuffie had cancer, but when I talked to him last, he said it was in remission. Tears burned my eyes as I thought the worst. My mentor, Don, reminded me to be careful of my imagination and to rest in the Lord. But I'd forgotten I had a refuge to turn to and God to fight my battles. So I rested in the shadow of the Almighty, surrendering my plans for his plans. God wanted me to have a lifestyle of always being aware of his protection, and he must have a reason he didn't want me to return to prison. On my knees, I prayed, asking God to show me his plans and calm me to wait for his answer. Shortly after, a peace washed over me as God reminded me of John 14:27: "Peace I leave with you; my peace I give you. I do not give to you as the world gives. Do not let your hearts be troubled and do not be afraid." That peace was his presence in me, and I wiped my tears away and smiled, knowing he held me in the palm of his hand. God will give you peace, too, no matter your situation, if you turn to him and accept his offer of grace, just like Nick and Luke did.

So what do I think happened to Luke? Why did Tyrone kill him? Was it part of a gang initiation?

I bumped into a former correction officer who'd worked at SCI Cresson, where Tyrone had been before it closed. He'd had several encounters with Tyrone while there. I shared my story and asked him if he thought Tyrone was part of a gang.

"No. And let me tell you why. Whenever there was trouble in the prison, guess who was in the middle? Tyrone—and he had a lot of enemies, so he wasn't part of a gang because of that. Gang members have many friends, not enemies. People have to like you to want you to join their group."

About a week before he died, Luke had talked to his lifelong friend, Dylan. Dylan told me Luke had said, "I'm going to keep my machete on me, and if anyone tries to take anything away from me, I'll use it to protect myself. If I die, I die. I'm tired of people taking advantage of me."

Even though this broke my heart, I believe my son was there to buy a gun from Tyrone. Tyrone was on edge because the deal wasn't completed in the house like the others, and Luke was a stranger to him. Luke was nervous about the whole situation. It was dusk, and they stood near a streetlight. With Tyrone and Luke not trusting each other, when Luke reached into the backpack to get his money out, Tyrone panicked. Pulling his gun from his waist, Tyrone had to take a step back so he could point the gun at Luke's head to shoot. Luke was gone in an instant. He felt no pain, and I doubt he saw it coming. If Luke saw anything, the gun only appeared for a second or two before the shooting. And the video my family saw proved this. They all confirmed that from the time Luke reached into the bag and the time the gun went off was about three seconds. I'd like to believe Luke didn't know anything was happening and woke to angels escorting him to heaven, where he met his great-grandma and Mike's mom. I don't know if his dad was a Christian, so I don't know if he was in heaven to meet Luke. But I know Jesus welcomed my son with open arms because Nick told me that my son was a Christian, and I will be forever grateful for that gift of peace. Nick will always hold a special place in my heart.

·♥·♥·♥·♥·♥·

My Transformational Journey

There are people God puts in my life for me to help them through their rough patches and lead them to him. And sometimes angels appear as strangers to help me, just like the people God used at the prison to help me get through one of the roughest days of my life. I don't know if I'll ever know the actual story about Luke's murder, but it doesn't matter.

Something that dawned on me when Luke was alive was how he'd turned his back on God as a teenager even though he'd accepted him as his Savior at seven. Because of that, every day became a battle since I was worried about him spending eternity in hell—he'd said he didn't believe there was a God. If Nick hadn't given me that gift of peace, I would continue with the unstoppable stress that ate me alive. I'd rather have my son gone and realize he was in heaven than have him alive and worry he will live in hell for all eternity when he dies. If he hadn't died, I wouldn't have known Jesus saved him. So I try to live as Dr. Suess said, "Don't cry because it's over; smile because it happened."

19. Fear on the Edge of a Cliff

Mike thought it was a good idea to test my limits since I'd been cycling for four months. But his test brought me to my knees. The Quemahoning Reservoir, or the Que, in Hooversville, PA, was a forty-minute drive from our house. The trail had a single track—a one-foot wide dirt path that meandered through trees, rocks, and along the cliffside with a beautiful view of the Que Creek below.

After parking the truck, Mike unloaded our mountain bikes. Even though we'd been completing road and gravel rides for which you usually use a road bike, I'd bought a mountain bike because it had wider tires, and I was very unsteady on the bike, even after months of riding. Sitting in a bent-over position was necessary because of the low handlebars. As I wasn't able to hold this position for long because of the agony the curves in my back had caused, Mike added a spacer to the handlebars, raising them four inches. That doesn't seem like much, but it made a world of difference. Occasionally, some riders flew down the road or smooth gravel trails, steering with their knees. They didn't need to hold their handlebars, but that was dangerous—not that I'd ever be good enough to do that.

After loading the water bottles onto our bikes, I mounted my phone in its holder and started Strava to record my ride. Strava is terrific because you can follow other riders and track your activity. It also keeps track of your accomplishments: personal records and local legends (the most rides in the last ninety days). If and when you have the best time over everyone, Strava gives you the title of king or queen of the mountain. Naturally, I wanted to be a queen.

After riding down a hill from the parking lot, I followed Mike onto the trailhead. The path twisted between beautiful trees as birds chirped, making me relax as I felt at one with nature. There were several segments on the trail. Most segments intersected with the road. We had just started one of them. Mike was ahead of me, and he looked back. "Gain speed so you can make it up the hill."

Listening to Mike, I flew around the corner and saw the hill and the curve before me as the wind whipped my hair. Zipping up the mountain, I panicked and didn't think I could make the turn, so I slammed on the brakes, falling sideways as I did. Catching myself before hitting the dirt, I pushed my bike up the rest of the hill because it was too steep to pedal. Remounting my bike at the top, I saw Mike ahead, waiting for me.

We climbed higher. And higher. I saw the glistening body of the Que through the trees below. The water reflected the mountains, so I stopped to take a picture. "Tammy, it gets steeper ahead. Let's turn around here."

"No, Mike. I'm scared to ride back down the mountain we just came up. Let's keep going." I should have listened to Mike because it only got worse.

Mike zipped ahead of me, and I tried to keep up. My body shook as I tried to steer my bike on the one-foot-wide path. There was a mountain to the right and a cliff to the left. The ridge leaned slightly, and there was a risk of injury if you went over the edge since there were many trees and rocks before the water at the bottom.

"Yikes!" My pedal hit the mountain on my right as I tried to hug it to stay away from the cliff. Realizing that was dangerous, I tried to stay in the middle of the path, but it was too small for my shaking body.

"No! Oh no!" My bike tilted sideways and threw me to the cliff's edge. My foot slipped in the dirt as I tried to catch myself before falling down the hill. Leaning forward, I pushed myself into the mountain, which was now one with my handlebar. Slowly, I pulled myself upright and maneuvered my body next to the hill, putting my bike near the edge of the drop-off.

Mike's voice echoed in the distance. "Are you OK back there?"

"I fell off my bike. This cliff is steep, and I'm scared to move."

"Do you need me to come back?"

"No. Just give me a minute." *What's Mike going to do? He can't even see me since he's around the curve.*

Please, God, don't let me fall down this mountain. I took several deep breaths before slowly pushing my bike along the path. The cliff looked less intimidating when riding because I was busy concentrating on steering my bike and didn't have time to look down. But now, it looked inevitable that I would eventually end up at the bottom.

Terrified, I continued pushing, knowing I needed to remount my bike or this would take hours. I knew I'd found my chance when I saw a strong-looking tree along the cliff's edge ahead. Since I was new to cycling, anytime I started pedaling, my hands shook, and I swerved left and right. So I knew I could use that tree to stop me from falling off the mountain if I went over the edge right there. Positioning my bike several feet from the tree, I sat on the seat, ready to face my fear. My heart pulsated in my fingertips. Taking a deep breath, I pushed off and pedaled as hard as possible to gain speed. The slower I rode, the less control I had of my bike, so I tried to pick up the pace while I had the advantage of my safety net—the tree. Success!

Riding along that tiny trail, I was more scared than ever, but I continued because I was too afraid to turn back. Now the one-foot path slanted steeply toward the sharp drop-off. Terrified, I let the tears flow, thinking I'd slide off the edge. There was no turning around. Fearing the unknown was easier than worrying about what I knew was behind me. Seeing a huge hill ahead of me made me pedal harder. Finally, the path turned right and away from the edge. I soon caught up to my husband, who was waiting for me.

He took one look at my face, and I'm sure he saw my fear. "I told you we should turn back a while ago."

"I know you did, but I was too afraid to go back down that hill. I'm never coming here again if I survive this ride." Thunder boomed in the distance as the sky grew dark.

Mike looked at the clouds. "We need to move. It's going to rain."

"My weather app says we're good for another hour. But it doesn't look that way." Pedaling hard, I followed Mike higher up the mountain through the green-leaved trees until we reached the summit. If I thought the cliffs scared me while ascending the hills, I didn't know how frightened I'd be going down the mountain. Briefly, I stopped. Then, taking a deep breath, my shaky hands steered my bike as I followed Mike along the trail. There was a steep U-shaped curve ahead. At the last minute, I jumped off my bike and walked around the turn. That was the worst decision I could have made because there wasn't enough room on the path for me and my bike. My tires pushed dirt over the trail's edge as I struggled to move, and I fought gravity as it tried to pull me into the trees and rocks below. When we merged onto the pavement at the bottom of the hill, I got on my knees and kissed the ground. And I have the picture and video to prove it.

As we sped down the road, I yelled to Mike, "I'm never coming back here!" Rain soaked us while we rode to the truck.

"I'm proud of you, Tammy. You faced your fears. I'll get you back here soon."

"No way!"

At the truck, Strava said we'd ridden over fourteen miles and climbed 900 feet. Wow! Proud of myself for my once-in-a-lifetime accomplishment, I vowed never to revisit the Quemahoning Reservoir. But there were other heights to conquer. *Do I have the strength to face them?*

·♥·♥·♥·♥·♥·

My Transformational Journey

God must have been with me. Otherwise, I would not have been able to get my bike going again along that cliff since I was too shaky every time I started my ride. Philippians 4:13 says, "I can do all this through him who gives me strength."

20. Being Alone Makes Me Brave

When editing my second book in the Journeys Through Life series, I couldn't get any work done at home because I was distracted. So I booked a trip to our time-share in Virginia over Mother's Day. Being alone on that particular holiday may not have been a wise choice. But sometimes, well, a lot of times, I don't think things through.

After checking in, I stared at the tree-covered mountains around me as my car climbed the twisting turns on the hill toward the condo. Five electrical towers stood above dirt-covered ski slopes. Instead of thinking about my son in heaven since he left me behind, I celebrated the holiday because my son will always be alive in my heart. Massanutten offered mothers a free chairlift ride for the holiday. Terrified the two other times I'd ridden the chairlift down the mountain with Mike and my sister, Jamie, I didn't think I could do it. The only reason I'd agreed was because Jamie, Mike, and I had walked the two miles of the challenging Ridge Trail, and we were exhausted, too tired to hike the additional long walk down the ski slope.

Figuring I'd test my hiking capabilities before attempting a solo hike on the difficult Ridge Trail, I hiked the Kaylors Knob Trail, a moderate hike in the opposite direction at the top of the mountain. My heart rate was 166 bpm for most of the walk. Constantly stopping and gasping for air should have told me to slow down. But no, I don't know how to do anything in a leisurely way. Everything has to be a competition, even if I'm only competing with myself.

I went up and down the hills, only catching my breath when I saw something worthy of a photo. There were Pink Lady Slippers everywhere. These orchids grow in the woodlands. Snapping pictures of other flowers, pinecones, and trees, I had to be careful not to trip on tree roots or rocks obstructing the dirt trail because I took several photos without stopping. After several close calls, my ankle hurt, and I felt like I'd sprained it. Still, I pushed on to the end of the trail.

Sweat dripped from my hair, and I swatted away flies as I climbed into my car after my hike. Chugging an entire container of water, I looked at Strava. I'd hiked almost four miles in two hours, climbing 621 feet.

When I returned to the condo, my body protested as I forced myself out of the car and up the three flights of stairs into the time-share. Finally, soaking in the Jacuzzi, I fell asleep. My muscles ached twenty-four hours later, and my calves cramped for two days, making walking hard. Oh, the pain.

Packing my backpack with three bottles of water and my phone, I set out in the late morning of day three to hike the difficult Ridge Trail. The trail scared me because I remember my husband pulling me to the top of steep climbs and holding my hands along the dangerous steep-edge drop-offs. But he wasn't here. And I would face my fears, as my book subtitle says: *Life Begins with Travel: Facing My Fears, Finding My Smile*. I just needed faith in myself—and in God.

After parking the car, I climbed many steps to start my four-mile hike from the scenic overlook at Massanutten's mountaintop. Many people sat at the trailhead, and I passed several groups returning to their cars. The beginning of the trail was easy. There were bushes to push through in parts and a few rocks to be careful of, but other than that, nothing hard. Today, I would take it slow.

Learning from my past mistakes, I put my long blond hair in a ponytail. That would hopefully keep me cool. The higher the trail went, the rockier the terrain became. It made me happy to take my time and enjoy the views through the trees instead of rushing. Whenever the trail meandered at the cliff's edge, I looked for other options and sometimes pushed through bushes so I didn't have to go near the edge.

Listening to audiobooks is one of my favorite things to do. Time flies when I get immersed in a good story, so I had one of my earbuds in. I didn't wear both because I needed to be aware of my surroundings. A sign at the entrance said that bears frequented the area. It advised me to stand my ground, wave sticks, or make noise if I encountered one. *Oh, please don't let that happen. I'll die of a heart attack if it does.* There were also rattlesnakes living under the rocks adorning the entire trail. My chance to back out had come and gone when I passed the sign that said the trail was rated as difficult.

At the top of one hill, there were so many rocks everywhere that I couldn't find the trail or any blue spray paint showing I was on the path. The cliff was to the left, so naturally, I descended the hill to the right. My butt slid down a few rocks since I couldn't find safe footing on the rugged terrain. I hoped a rattlesnake didn't bite me. There were plenty of crevices between the stones. After sliding down a rock, my foot slipped into a hole when I tried to stand. Crying out in pain, I hoped my ankle was OK. I hadn't seen anyone on the trail for a long time, so I was worried I was alone. But I wanted to make my husband proud of me. And that meant I had to finish. My vision blurred as I pushed back tears from the pain.

Other than a few scrapes on my skin, my foot and leg appeared fine. Ascending halfway up the next rocky hill, I still couldn't find the trail. After looking everywhere, I continued to the top of the ridgeline, where an impressive view of the Blue Ridge Mountains in the distance greeted me. Hoping that being higher would show the way, I was disappointed. Lost. There wasn't a path anywhere. So I followed the ridge and went down the hill, pushing through bushes. Something ran next to my feet. I screamed and almost fell. My watch showed my heartbeat was up to 163 bpm. There were noises all around me, but nothing that sounded like a bear or a rattlesnake, so I continued.

At the top of the next hill was a cliff to the left and a slightly steep drop-off to the right. Even though I couldn't see the trail, I remembered Mike had pulled me over a massive rock on a slant along the cliff. A two-inch raised edge in the rock's bottom was the only thing to keep me from sliding over the edge to my death. The lip went the whole way across the stone. Too busy trying to find a way through the maze, I hadn't realized how close to the edge I was.

Sitting on a rock with my backpack next to the edge, I drank my water, trying to stop the spinning that had begun. No longer feeling safe on the rocky ledge, I knew I needed to move. *How am I going to stand up and not fall over the edge? Shall I put my backpack on while sitting or hold it in my hand? Are people really crazy enough to do these death-defying stunts?* Knowing I wasn't brave enough to walk on the slanted rock, I'd need to backtrack. Turning around was my only option.

As I did so, a shot rang out in the distance. *Who's shooting? And why? It's not hunting season yet.* It reminded me of a time my mom called.

"Tammy, I turned the car left in Hornerstown. I hear shots ahead of me, but I can't see where they're coming from."

"Mom, what are you doing in that part of town?" Both Mom and I knew Hornerstown was a dangerous neighborhood where many drug deals and shootings took place.

"I'm going to the doctor. I don't know if I should pull over or keep driving."

"Where are the sounds coming from? Do you see any cop cars?"

"No. I think the shots are only one block away. The way I'm heading."

"Pull over, Mom!"

"Do you think I should get out of the car?"

"No. But duck below the dash in case a bullet comes your way."

"OK."

I heard the terror in her voice. Then I heard a gunshot. "Mom, are you ducking?"

"Yes. I'm scared."

"Can you turn around? Get out of there."

Mom left quickly. We watched the news for the next several days, but we never heard what happened.

Losing Luke was hard. Unbearable. I wasn't strong enough to lose my mother too. I loved her dearly. She was always there to help and comfort me when I needed her. I can't imagine life without her, so I'm glad she was OK and didn't get murdered like Luke.

I'd made it almost two-thirds of the way to the end of my hike but failed. As I passed a tall, muscular man five minutes after I had turned around, I explained to him what had happened and how dangerous it was. He said he'd be fine, and I considered asking if I could join him. *But will he care enough about me to help me over the cliff's edge? And, more importantly, do I trust him enough not to let me fall?* I needed to return to my car.

Strava said I'd climbed 401 feet in under two hours and walked almost four miles. When I returned to the condo, my legs didn't hurt as badly as last time. This time, I even walked the garbage down the three flights of stairs to the dumpster before showering. It was challenging to look at my body for ticks since my husband and I always checked each other. It's necessary because there were many where we lived, and once, we found one on Mike. But I did my best, although I couldn't check the back of my head.

Beginning the hike, I'd hoped to walk to the trail's end. Then I could have ridden the chairlift down. So I decided to do the chairlift ride anyway to conquer another fear. Preparing myself for my upcoming trip to Glacier National Park, MT, and Golden, Canada, where I would visit six national parks in the Rocky Mountains with my friend, was at the top of my list. Elfriede had said we would take a gondola over the forest to the top, where I could see six mountain ranges. So I needed to practice getting over my fear of heights.

The man behind the counter at the General Store handed me a free ticket when I told him I had a son in heaven—that qualified me as a mother for the free access. He wanted to know more about my story, so I gave him a bookmark with the link to my website and told him about my first memoir, *Gone in an Instant*. He said he'd buy a copy, and I left. My body shook as I walked to the bottom of the ski slope. I babbled to the poor attendant who took my ticket; he was kind and told me I'd be fine. I'm a talker when I'm nervous. The attendant encouraged me to enjoy the views. He said he had faith in me. How kind of him. *Can I do this?*

Pressing on, I stood on the yellow feet markers to wait as the chair swung around the turn on the cables. My butt plopped in the middle of the seat, big enough for four people. *Tammy, you got this. You are stronger than you think.* Pulling my phone out of my fanny pack, I called Mike.

"Mike, can you see me?"

"No. I'm not looking at my phone."

"Well, look."

"What? Oh my. Are you on a chairlift? I'm so jealous."

"Mike, I did it!"

"That's great! Say hi to John." Mike pointed the camera at his brother before turning it back on himself. "Did you call me because you're afraid and want a distraction?"

"No. I called so you could be proud of me for facing my fear. I'm not afraid."

"That's great. I'm so happy for you."

"Oh, wow. The chair stopped, and it's swinging." My shaking hand almost dropped the phone.

Either Mike or his brother said, "It probably broke down. You're stuck up there."

But my nerves had already calmed. "It's OK. I'll just lie on the seat until they fix it." I was getting more comfortable by the minute.

Whenever someone got on the lift, they momentarily stopped the cables. The more they stopped to let people on, the more I relaxed and enjoyed the swinging. I didn't want it to end. What a Mother's Day I had, even if I was alone—although Luke was with me in spirit, and I knew he was proud of me for not only facing my fear but conquering it.

·♥·♥·♥·♥·♥·

My Transformational Journey

Sometimes the more I do something, the less I'm afraid. The first two times I rode the chairlift, I was terrified. But the third time, I liked it. It's kind of like trying new foods. They say you have to try something at least seven times before you'll like it. Growing up, I never ate vegetables. Now I eat broccoli, cauliflower, and tomatoes. And it all started with trying it for the first time. And then a second.

The other thing I learned is that when someone else was with me, and I was afraid, I leaned on them. And when I voiced my fears, that made me more scared. So facing my fears alone may be the way to go. Maybe I can overcome my fear of heights if I keep pushing myself. But I'm still unsure if I want to cycle at the Que again. That was dangerous. I'm not a daredevil—at least not yet. But maybe someday I will be.

21. WILL I DIE TRYING?

Tyrone finally sent me a letter. He was in the hole (Restrictive Housing Unit) for something frivolous, or so he said, and when he got out, he would be transferred to another prison. He wished me a happy Mother's Day, which I thought was kind. My son's killer said he never received my book, so I sent him another through Amazon. Hopefully, he would receive it. A month later, Tyrone called and said his dad had read and loved my book. I hope Tyrone eventually gets a copy and reads my story.

Since cycling cleared my mind from stress, I asked Mike to take me to Ghost Town Trail, which starts in Ebensburg, Pennsylvania. It's a thirty-two-mile ride downhill to Saylor Park in Blacklick. But then you must fight to ride back up that slight hill, so Mike didn't want to ride too far. But I pushed him, and we rode thirty miles before Mike stopped because he was worried. Even with my padded shorts, my butt was black and blue from riding several days in a row, but I'm a fighter.

My husband took my car to work the next morning, so I had access to his truck. Sneaking around the house while Mike messed around in the garage until it was time to leave for work, I packed my water bottles and backpack with all intentions of showing my husband what my body was capable of. Who cared if WJAC TV predicted the temperature would reach 90° that day. I was invincible! As soon as I saw my car zip down the road, I implemented my plan. I loaded my bike and backpack and set the navigation to Saylor Park. *Just wait and see, Mike. I'll make you proud!*

Unloading the bike was a challenge. After trying to lift it three times, I conceded it was too heavy. No one was around except for the lawn care worker, who was busy cutting the grass in the baseball field. Inspiration struck. After climbing into the truck bed, I easily lowered my bike to the ground while the blazing sun warned me of what was soon to come. After a quick restroom stop after my almost one-hour drive, I hit the trail.

About ten miles and one hour later, a few men stopped ahead of me. Sweat dripped down my chin, and the back of my hair was already soaked. "Hello. Why'd you stop?" They pointed at an animal in the middle of the flat dirt trail. A porcupine stood there like he didn't have a care in the world. Climbing off my bike, I drank over half my water as my legs screamed in pain.

"He's been there for twenty minutes," the man who introduced himself as a priest said.

I scratched my head deep in thought. "Can porcupines do any damage to people or bike tires?"

"Not sure. Maybe." The taller man in a tank top removed his green ball cap.

I made a video and took a picture.

"I'm heading out." The priest climbed onto his bike.

"Mind if I ride with you?" I shoved my water bottle back into my pack.

We all pulled out together, and I stayed as far away from the porcupine as possible. It darted at the priest once before slowly waddling off the path.

Letting the men talk amongst themselves, I only spoke when they asked me a question. My legs were cramping, and I pushed myself to the max to keep up. It must have been 80° already, and I chugged more water every time we stopped. When we reached Dilltown, I watched the taller man ride toward his car, yelling goodbye as he did.

I tied my hair up in a ponytail. My face and shoulders were at the mercy of my sunscreen since there weren't any trees above me as I tried to pedal faster to catch up to the priest who wasn't waiting for me. By the time I reached him, we were back in the shade, and it was more comfortable. My heart pounded. My chest ached. Looking at my watch, I saw my heart rate was 170 bpm. That was way too high. No wonder I had trouble breathing—I knew I had to stop again.

"Your face is red. Are you OK?" The priest took a drink out of his water bottle.

After catching my breath, I told him about my memoir and how my son was murdered.

"Most people wouldn't dare forgive their child's killer. Why'd you do it?"

"Because Jesus forgave me for my sins, so what right do I have not to forgive someone who sins against me?"

"You're right. Colossians 3:13 says to forgive as the Lord forgave you."

I wiped the sweat from my forehead and thought about something Billy Graham had said. "Perhaps the most glorious word in the English language is forgiveness."

"Besides," I said to the priest, "if I didn't forgive him, the stress of that unforgiveness and the hatred would eat me alive."

"You're a wise woman."

My heart rate had slowed, so I started pedaling again. My head pounded, and I barely heard the priest when he said goodbye three miles later. Sitting on a bench, I ate my peanut butter sandwich and drank a few gulps of warm water to wash it down. The ice had long ago melted in my Contigo bottle that was supposed to keep drinks cold for over twenty-four hours. My WJAC news weather app said the temperature was 92°, and every muscle in my body ached. Even my hands. *Why did I think I could do this?* I'd gotten close to my son's longtime friend, Dylan, since Luke had passed. Crying, I called to ask him to come and get me. But he said he was out of town, and I couldn't think of anyone else with a truck except my dad. And I didn't want a lecture, so a call to him was out of the question. Fatigue overcame my body, and I knew I was in trouble. But I wasn't willing to admit it to anyone. At least not yet.

Starting to pedal, I tried to think positive thoughts. Tears poured down my face as I reached twenty-two miles. I was light-headed, and my mouth was dry. When I tried to use the restroom, nothing came out. It had been over five hours since I had last peed. *But I am strong; I can finish this ride!*

My bike moved so slowly that I was surprised I didn't fall over. Whenever I passed cyclists coming from the other direction, I quickly wiped my tears away and pasted a smile on my face while they passed as I said a weak hello. As soon as they passed, I cried and rested my elbows on the handlebars as I tried to continue. Looking at passing cars on the road up the hill through the trees, I contemplated climbing the incline and flagging a truck for a ride. I was getting desperate, and I still had ten miles to go. Common sense told me I should have turned around ten miles ago and rode downhill back to the truck.

When I arrived in Nanty Glo, I stopped at a bar along the trail. As I entered, I looked in my wallet for my credit card and realized that I had forgotten both the credit card and cash in my haste and excitement. Back to my bike, I went. I'd forgotten that Mike had a signal through the app I used and knew exactly where I was.

After I'd ridden another six long, exhausting miles, my phone rang. "Are you OK?"

"No! I'm not."

"Let me come get you."

"OK."

"I expected an argument. That tells me you're not well."

"I'm sick. I fell off my bike a little way back. My body aches, and my lips and hands are trembling."

"That's not good. Can you make it to Ebensburg? I can see you on the app, and you don't have far to go."

"Yes."

"Call me when you're there or if you can't make it."

We hung up, and I pushed on, knowing my face and shoulders were burning since there weren't any trees on that portion of the trail. Too tired to put on more sunscreen, I chose to pay the consequences. Finally, I arrived in Ebensburg and called Mike. His boss let him leave work early as I almost passed out on a picnic table waiting for him to arrive. He had to take both tires off my bike to get them in the trunk, and it took an hour for me to recover from what I'd put my body through as we drove to pick up the truck, which I had to drive home.

·♥·♥·♥·♥·♥·

My Transformational Journey

Even though I wanted to push myself and prove I could ride sixty-four miles, I should've chosen a cooler day and ensured I had cash and a credit card. What I did was stupid, and I could have died or ended up in the hospital. So in the future, I needed to think with my brain, not my ego. When I got home, my body gave out, and I slept for twelve hours. Waking up the following day, I discovered my black and blue butt had rubbed raw in spots because I wasn't used to riding for that length of time. My head still pounded, and I must have drunk a gallon of water to recover.

22. Mom, Do You Want to Keep the Bat as a Pet?

My phone rang. Mom was out of breath. "Tammy, come over. Hurry! There's a bat in the house. We need help."

Dad was out of town for work, and my mom and sister were at the house.

Mom was awakened by my sister screaming. "Help! Mom! Help!"

Mom said she had no idea what was happening, so she ran to my sister's bedroom, thinking an intruder was in the house. Her heart pounded as she tripped in her haste, racing toward the door. Her hand shook as she twisted the doorknob. Jamie was shaking on the bed, staring into the face of a terrifying-looking bat that dared her to make a move. Mom told Jamie to slide back across the bed slowly. The winged beast flew, trying to hit its target in the head. My mom grabbed my sister's arm and pulled her off the bed, practically dragging Jamie to a corner of the room.

"Jamie, grab our hats from the closet. Hurry! I can see its teeth!" Mom cried as the bat squealed out of the bedroom. Downstairs, Mom panicked. "Jamie, get me a towel. I must get it off the coffee table and shoo it out the door. Bats carry germs and diseases, spreading them on everything they touch."

Mom ducked as Jamie ran to the kitchen. After she was in the clear, she swung the door open, but her nightmare got worse when the bat flew back upstairs.

"Mom! I'm here!" I ran into the house without taking off my sneakers. The sight that greeted me left me in shock. Pillows covered the floor. The contents of an emptied garbage can littered the couch. Used paper towels and tissues lay on the beige carpet that still had vacuum lines. Mom had a nightgown on with a straw hat on her head, and sweat ran over her forehead. Jamie wore pajamas and a Mexican birthday hat. I remembered she got it when we took her to the restaurant for her birthday.

After regaining my composure, I fought my fear. "Where is it? What can I do? My friend had one in her house, and she opened all the doors and windows until it flew out."

"All the windows have screens in." Mom started up the steps.

I followed. "Why do you have a kitchen towel?"

"I'm trying to shoo it out the door."

"What? That's crazy. Where's your broom?"

Jamie left us and ran to get it.

At the top of the steps, Mom and I peeked around the corner. I jumped when I heard a clicking noise. I almost fell down the steps as my mom backed into me. Goosebumps formed on my arms and legs, and the hair on my arms stood up.

"I think it's in Jamie's room again." Mom crept down the hall, and I followed as Jamie walked up behind me.

"Give me the broom!" Jamie handed it to me as she backed up several feet and disappeared onto the steps around the corner. I followed Mom into the bedroom. The bat was lying on the bed.

"Would you look at that?" Mom's eyes were huge as she stared at the impressive details on a creature we'd never seen up close before. The brown skin was deeply veined, and I could see my sister's purple bedspread through the wings, wings that were lined with pinkish arms and legs. Those pink legs ended in foot bones, and the creature must have been almost a foot long. Pointy ears stood over its beady eyes and furry brown, cute face. It reminded me of a hamster.

"Look out!" Mom screamed as she hit the floor. The creature flew over her head and almost hit me in the face as I tried to shove it out the door with the broom.

"Ew. It grazed my shoulder. Disgusting. A minute ago, I thought it was cute." I tried to brush the germs off my shoulder. "How do you think it got in?"

"Probably through the attic vents. Then it squeezed under the bedroom door. I wish your dad were here. He'd know what to do."

"We're never going to get rid of him. Are you sure you don't want to keep the bat as a pet?"

Mom gave me a look that said I was trying her patience.

Jamie was in the living room, too scared to join us. "It's down here by the door! Hurry!"

By the time I ran downstairs, it took off, flying through the house back up the stairs. We weren't able to find it. So I guess it found a way outside on its own, or it would make another appearance when we least expected it.

We cleaned everything it touched. Mom felt sick the next two days just thinking about her contaminated house.

Jamie told us later that a mouse scratching in the attic had awakened her. When she reached for the light, the glow from her alarm clock had illuminated the bat, sitting with two beady eyes staring at her. "I couldn't move. That's when I screamed for Mom to help."

"We've been having trouble with mice lately." Mom looked at me when I made a disgusted face.

"I caught one in a trap in the basement a few days ago. But it was still alive. I didn't want to touch it, so I called my friend Brian, who lives a block away." Jamie shivered at the memory.

Mom, Jamie, and I hugged. Tight. That was a bonding moment for our family, but without my dad. Not that he would've hugged us anyway.

•❤•❤•❤•❤•❤•

My Transformational Journey

Even though I was terrified, I knew I had to help my mom and sister for all those years when my mom took care of me. And I wasn't the easiest child to raise. I'd caused her a lot of stress, so I tried to make her life easier by helping when she needed anything. After all, that's what family is supposed to do.

After apologizing for all the trouble I'd put her through many years ago, our relationship had healed, and we loved each other deeply. And my sister and I had always been close, even though there were five years between us. Dad was a different story. It took a lot to get him to give a compliment or a hug.

23. Why Did I Write This Book?

Whenever we lose a loved one, it feels like our life is over. But it's not. Maybe the best way to go on living without our loved ones is to keep them alive in our hearts and find them in as many places and things as we can. If there's a slim chance my lost loved ones can hear me, I'll keep talking to them.

How about you? Are you one of those people like me who needs to know every detail about something that happened? At Tyrone's sentencing, he said there was more to the story. I moved heaven and earth and didn't find anything new. But I've learned that when I feel depressed or stressed, it's best if I keep busy. Whether I exercise, cook, clean, travel, sing worship songs, or hang out with loved ones, it all helps. That's how I've dealt with my loss and inability to learn all the details of Luke's murder. And maybe sometimes, we need to let peace take over instead of searching for answers. I've come out the other side stronger because I looked deep inside myself and learned that God loves me just as I am—broken or not.

God's greatest commands are to love him and to love others. Tyrone reached out again after he finally received my book. It was the second one I'd sent, and it took more than a month for him to get it. His voice was soft on the call. He sounded depressed when he again said he was sorry for the loss he had caused me. "I read *Gone in an Instant* two times already, and I'm going to reread it, Miss Tammy."

"Wow! That's great. Did you get my letter?"

"What letter?"

"I sent a letter the day the book arrived at the prison to tell you I had a visit scheduled for next Thursday. It was important that you read the book before I visit."

"I didn't get a letter."

"Maybe you will. If not, I'll be there next Thursday unless something goes wrong and I don't make it through security."

"OK. I can't wait to see you. My five minutes are up. I gotta go."

A recording said, "The caller has disconnected from the call."

Tyrone called again the following day since I kept money in an account so he could call whenever he wanted. His voice was low, and he sounded sad, like he'd been crying.

"I know how much you loved Luke, and I'm sorry he's gone. You truly loved him and did everything you could for him. I wish I were blessed with a mother like you. My mom was never a part of my life and wanted nothing to do with me when I met her a few times when I was sixteen."

"I'm so sorry, Tyrone. Did she give you a reason?"

"No. But I saw her a few other times, and she wouldn't talk with me." He explained her problems to me, but that is his story to tell. And he would like to write a book someday.

"My dad had his own issues, but eventually influenced me later in life." Again, he told me what the issues were, but I'm not comfortable sharing them without permission from everyone involved.

"My grandmother raised my sisters and me before she sent me and one of my sisters to DHS—the Pennsylvania Department of Human Services. You might know it as Child Welfare Services. My dad didn't come back into my life until later."

"Sorry, I didn't know, Tyrone."

"I'd love to share my story with you. There's so much I have to tell you."

"I can't wait to hear it."

"I'm looking forward to our visit. Do you know I've been in prison for almost six years, and you're the only one who has ever visited me?"

"That's terrible."

"Time's up. I've got to go."

Sitting at the table, I cried. My heart broke for Tyrone, and I wondered if he had ever felt loved. *Since his gram raised him and later sent him away, how did that make him feel?* After twenty minutes, I finally dried my eyes and said I was done crying. But that wasn't to be.

A few hours later, I received an email saying the prison had canceled my visit. I looked online at the visitation schedule, but there weren't any openings for the next sixty days. I knew Tyrone had gotten into trouble again. On yesterday's call, Tyrone had said the money from his SCI Camp Hill account didn't transfer to the new prison. He needed deodorant and shampoo. The prison only gave them soap.

"It's tough on your skin and dries it out. I was so desperate for money that I got caught when I tried to make liquor to sell."

Knowing he needed money, I'd considered putting some on his account, but the last time I did, my credit card hit me with so many additional fees that I wanted to wait and do it in person when I visited the prison. Also, I discussed it with my husband because I knew he would disagree with me giving Tyrone money when we struggled with our own bills. But my heart broke for him, and I wondered what it was like deep inside prison walls.

A few weeks after my visit, Tyrone's previous cellmate at another prison sent me a letter. Darrell said, "I've read your book *Gone in an Instant*. All my life, I've been searching for the comfort that most people have coming into this world. To be accepted and loved by somebody. Anybody. Since reading your book, I've realized that forgiveness is the key to the recipe of life. The guards here at SCI Huntingdon also read parts of your book."

Wow! I'm making a difference. My books are changing lives. That's all I want out of life—to use the gifts God has given me by sharing my story to help others find their way to heaven.

Many nights after Tyrone had murdered Luke, I thought about what might have been. What if it had been my son who killed Tyrone instead of vice versa? Would I be able to survive without seeing Luke? How much money would I need to give Luke each month so he could live as comfortably as possible? Could I afford it? Tyrone had said how noisy prison was and that sleeping was difficult. Old radiators made his room excruciatingly hot, and the walls of his five-by-six-foot cell were soaked because of it. There was only room for bunk beds, a small desk, a sink, and a toilet. "Imagine going to the bathroom with someone a few feet away," he'd said to me on my visit. That would have been my undoing.

Would Luke have ended up in the hole all the time like Tyrone? Or would he have been a model citizen, followed the rules, and received an early release like he had from rehab?

Anyway, I've thought long and hard about the situation with Tyrone. I've come to care deeply for him. And I will continue to do so. As I've told Tyrone, I will continue to visit him and take his calls as long as he'll have me. I genuinely want to help him become a better person. But he must take the first step and want to better himself. Until then, I will continue to forgive the unforgivable and love the unlovable.

Do you know anyone who has had a challenging life or hasn't felt loved? Is there a way you can help them feel your love, or can you share Jesus with them so they can feel the love of the only true Savior? Regardless of whether you're a Christian, as the great Pastor Charles Stanley once said, "Every person is born with a deep desire to be loved unconditionally, but when this yearning is not fully met, many hurts and scars can result. What security and wholeness there is in knowing that we can call God 'our Father' and receive that unconditional love!"

·♥·♥·♥·♥·♥·

My Transformational Journey

The Bible says that love "keeps no record of wrongs" in 1 Corinthians 13:5. And Isaiah 43:18-19 says, "Forget the former things; do not dwell on the past." By choosing to forgive Tyrone for the hurt he caused, I freed myself from the potential anger I might once have felt. But could I forgive *and* forget? If I hadn't first forgiven him, forgetting would have become impossible. So even though his actions hurt me, I try to live as if I have no memory of the wrong I've suffered. But it's hard because Luke is missing from my daily life, so I continue to do my best to live like Jesus when he forgave his murderers on the cross. This is only possible because when I accepted Jesus as my Savior, God sent the Holy Spirit to live in me. And since it's God's nature to love, this enabled me to love Tyrone, whereas, before salvation, I would have found that impossible.

Because everyone wants to feel loved.

Even a stalker.

Even a murderer.

And even me.

·♥·♥·♥·♥·♥·

Want to follow Tammy as she travels, finding adventure one journey at a time, even if it involves meeting a killer in court or prison, visiting national parks, or seeing gorgeous beaches? Click or type https://mybook.to/TammyHorvath into your internet search bar to catch up with the first book or see all books in the Journeys Through Life memoir series.

Gone in an Instant: Losing My Son. Loving His Killer.

When a police officer knocks on Tammy Horvath's door and tells her that her son has been murdered, her life is shattered. As she struggles to come to terms with his death, a voice tells her to forgive his killer. In *Gone in an Instant*, will God reveal himself and set her free in a way she could never have imagined? Or will Tammy's spirit forever remain broken by one man's deed?

·♥·♥·♥·♥·♥·

If you enjoyed *Deep Inside*, please consider leaving a review to help other readers find a book they will love. You can submit a review wherever you find my book, even if you didn't buy it there. Just a few words will make a huge difference.

Just click or type the link below into your internet search bar.

Amazon review link: https://www.amazon.com/review/create-review?& asin=B0CTYN3R77

Goodreads review link: https://www.goodreads.com/book/show/2033 19035-deep-inside

IN CASE YOU MISSED IT—ALSO BY TAMMY HORVATH

Gone in an Instant: Losing My Son. Loving His Killer. **Book 1**

A son killed by a single bullet. A mother's heart shattered. As Tammy Horvath struggles to come to terms with her son's death, a voice tells her to forgive his killer.

With her soul tormented by the loss of her son, Tammy fights to get out of bed every day because she can't face a seemingly hopeless future. But Luke would want her to be happy. So she pushes forward and embarks on a journey, searching for peace, hope, and a chance to keep her son alive in her heart.

Will God reveal himself and set her free in a way she could never have imagined? Or will Tammy's spirit remain broken by one man's deed?

Life Begins with Travel: Facing My Fears. Finding My Smile. **Book 2**

A husband dead in a fiery crash. A son claimed by a killer's hand. Tammy Horvath doesn't think she'll ever smile again.

Strengthened by her faith, she bravely heads solo to Iceland to see the northern lights, where she climbs glaciers and ventures into caves before seizing the opportunity to travel more often.

Tammy will take you on a journey of love, laughter, and inspirational life lessons as she swims in the crystal-clear Caribbean Sea, gets stuck atop one of

Mexico's pyramids, endures a tropical storm in the Bahamas, and hikes amid Yellowstone National Park's spectacular scenery.

Will life's tragedies make Tammy cower in fear forever? Or can she embrace a world of adventure and find happiness again?

Deep Inside: Forgiving the Unforgivable. Loving the Unlovable. Book 3

A chilling behind-bars encounter with a killer unfolds. Step into the heart-wrenching world of his victim's grieving mother. Can the unforgivable be forgiven?

As Tammy Horvath grapples with the weight of depression following her profound loss, she discovers that no amount of exercise can completely mend her shattered soul. The quest for genuine healing takes a courageous turn as she confronts the murderer, unraveling the haunting mysteries behind Luke's tragic death.

Are the roots of Tammy's faith deep enough to make a difference? Or are Tammy's friends right in warning her against facing a cold-blooded killer?

Exploring Mountains and Beaches: Journeys Beyond Borders. Adventures Worth Pursuing. Book 4

What do you hold dear in life? For Tammy Horvath, it's the relentless pursuit of connecting with others, exploring new horizons alive with wonder, and seizing every moment while she checks off items on her bucket list.

As Tammy explores mountains and beaches in paradise, she's fueled by the allure of new cultures, creating memories that have made her who she is today. Throughout her island adventures to the Bahamas, Turks and Caicos, and Curacao, as well as hikes through national parks in the Canadian Rocky Mountains, surprises lurk at every turn—from navigating floods to fending off avian ambushes. Embracing the chaos, Tammy turns each misadventure into a story worth telling.

Join Tammy on this journey beyond borders, where each step brings her closer to the beauty of life.

One Text Away: A Doctor's Indecent Proposal. **Book 5**

In this true story, Tammy Horvath faces an indecent proposal from a respected younger doctor while she grapples with an unrelated daunting health scare: a breast lump that grows larger, demanding immediate action. Tammy must confront her deepest fears and let faith be her compass, forgiveness her guide, and self-discovery her destination.

Will the doctor's enticing compliments threaten Tammy's resolve to remain a faithful wife, causing her to destroy her marriage? Or will she have enough self-control to resist Adonis's charm?

Click or type https://mybook.to/TammyHorvath into your internet search bar, then choose a book to purchase an eBook, paperback, or audiobook of any book in the series recorded by Tammy Horvath. All books are available on Kindle Unlimited.

NOTE TO THE READER

About the Author

Author and speaker Tammy Horvath was born and raised on a floodplain in western Pennsylvania, where she currently resides with her amazing husband Michael. She has three wonderful adult stepchildren, along with her only child Luke, who is now in heaven with his Creator and finally at peace.

Tammy has almost three decades of administrative experience in real estate and insurance. She has volunteered for more than a decade with a Christian nonprofit providing education and other essential needs for at-risk children around the world. She has been a spokesperson for the nonprofit's needs, served in church ministries, and is always available to share her story and God's message of love and forgiveness.

Tammy and her husband still live in the same house where they raised Luke, even though she cries every time she enters his room.

Tammy will never stop grieving the loss of her only son Luke to a murderer's bullet. But she lives and writes with the assurance that she will see him again and that God will ultimately use her son's death for good. She loves sharing treasured memories of her son with anyone who will listen.

Tammy has written five books in the Journeys Through Life memoir series:

Remember that one person who hurt you, the one you can't forgive? In her first book, ***Gone in an Instant***, Tammy tells the heartbreaking story of losing her son to a murderer's bullet and the road she traveled to forgive his killer. Being vulnerable about her past and her mistakes helps readers start to explore their own. The last few chapters reveal a pathway to overcome failures and find freedom, just like Tammy did. It took time, but recently, she's been visiting Tyrone in prison. As a perfectionist, Tammy refuses to give up on anyone—even a murderer.

How do you attempt to escape what has caused you the most pain? Despite thump-in-the-stomach-harrowing challenges, Tammy's second book, *Life Begins with Travel*, reveals how embarking on a courageous journey to new destinations can cultivate emotional healing. Travel became the coping mechanism that she needed. Conquering her fears as she shares the smells, the tastes, the bumps and bruises acquired on her travels changed her and helped keep Tammy from getting stuck on the top of pyramids as she did in Mexico. The one irreconcilable truth from these stories is that travel is always transformational.

How do you navigate the suffocating weight of depression that follows a life-changing loss? A coroner's knock on Tammy's door changes her life forever. In her third book, *Deep Inside*, she tries to escape the pain through exercise. But to experience genuine healing, she must summon the courage to face the man who murdered Luke to unravel the haunting mysteries behind her son's tragic death. But only if she can pass the prison's high-tech security protocols. Are Tammy's friends right in warning her against facing a cold-blooded killer?

Do you have a bucket list that involves travel? Tammy loves to seize the moment and live life to the full by immersing herself in new cultures, feeling the warm sand between her toes on stunning beaches, and marveling at the grandeur of the Canadian Rockies' majestic mountains. Join Tammy on this thrilling journey where chaos awaits, and each misadventure unfolds into unforgettable tales in her fourth book, *Exploring Mountains and Beaches*.

Have you ever been tempted to have an affair? When a breast lump grows exponentially in one year, the doctor demands a biopsy. While dealing with stress, Tammy wrestles with the demons of insecurity when a handsome young doctor tries to sweep her off her feet. Like an addicted gambler, she considers putting it all in and betting on the win to satisfy her lust. Prepare to be captivated as Tammy navigates the shadows of doubt, trying to emerge into the light of hope in **One Text Away**, book five in the Journeys Through Life series.

Ultimately, Tammy writes and speaks so that every reader may know God's immeasurable love and that forgiveness is the essence of God's love. She can't wait for the day she meets God face-to-face and is reunited with her son and other loved ones in heaven.

Click or type https://mybook.to/TammyHorvath into your internet search bar, then choose a book to purchase an eBook, paperback, or audiobook of any book in the series recorded by Tammy Horvath. All books are available on Kindle Unlimited.

Chat with the author and other memoir authors and readers by joining the friendly, fun Facebook group We Love Memoirs at https://www.faceb ook.com/groups/welovememoirs/.

www.ingramcontent.com/pod-product-compliance
Lightning Source LLC
Chambersburg PA
CBHW030106070426
42448CB00037B/1051